*As this book is going to press, the airwaves are filled with stories upon stories of millions fleeing warfare and internal strife. To the countless refugees and displaced persons, in Rwanda, Bosnia, Haiti and elsewhere throughout the worlds of the ten directions, this book is respectfully dedicated. May they always dwell in the Pure Land of their Mind.*

## COVER ILLUSTRATION

**The Buddha surrounded by Bodhisattvas**

*Tun-Huang Cave 17, China*
*8th century*

Books by J.C. Cleary

*The Blue Cliff Record* (co-author), 1977.
*Swampland Flowers*, 1977.
*Zen Lore from the Source Mirror*, 1979.
*Zen Dawn*, 1986.
*A Buddha from Korea*, 1988.
*Zibo: The Last Great Zen Master of China*, 1989.
*Worldly Wisdom: Confucian Teachings from the Ming Dynasty*, 1991.
*A Tune Beyond the Clouds: Zen Teachings from Old China*, 1991.
*Meditating with Koans*, 1992
*Zen Letters: Teachings of Yuanwu*, 1994
*Recorded Sayings of Linji*
*Wumen's Barrier*

---

# J.C. Cleary

The translator of this volume holds a Ph.D. in East Asian Languages and Civilizations from Harvard University. He has translated a number of Zen and Confucian texts including, as co-author, the voluminous *Blue Cliff Record (Pi Yen Lu)*, a well-known collection of some one hundred koans selected from the Zen classic of all times, *Transmission of the Lamp*.

# PURE LAND
# PURE MIND

*The Buddhism of Masters*
*Chu-hung and Tsung-pen*

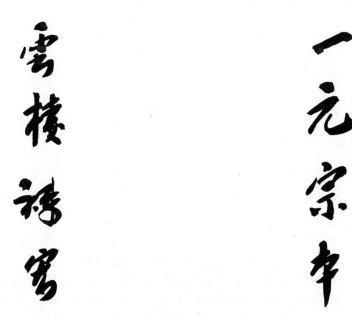

*Translated by*
**J . C .  Cleary**

*Foreword, Notes and Glossary*
*by Van Hien Study Group*

**SUTRA TRANSLATION COMMITTEE OF**
**THE UNITED STATES AND CANADA**
*New York - San Francisco - Toronto*
1994

This volume consists of excerpts from two Chinese Buddhist commentaries: *The Collected Works of Master Yun-ch'i Chu-hung* (Vn. *Chu Hoằng/Liên-Trì*; Jpn. *Unsei Shuko*) and *Direct Pointing Back to the Source* by Master I-yuan Tsung-pen (Vn. *Qui Nguyên Trực Chỉ / Nhất-Nguyên Tông-Bổn*). These texts, well-known in East Asia, appear here in English translation for the first time.

Reprinted for free distribution by
**The Corporate Body of the Buddha Educational Foundation**
11F., 55 Hang Chow South Road Sec 1, Taipei, Taiwan, R.O.C.
Tel: 886-2-23951198 , Fax: 886-2-23913415
Email: overseas@budaedu.org.tw

# About the Authors

**Master Chu-hung** (1535-1615), also known as Yün-ch'i or Lien-ch'ih, was (along with Han-shan Te-ch'ing and Tzu-po Chen-k'o) one of the three "dragon-elephants" or most illustrious monks of the Ming period. Together, they were responsible for the revival of Buddhism in sixteenth century China, a revival which still influences Buddhism today.

Trained as a monk in both the Zen and Pure Land traditions, Master Chu-hung emphasized strict observance of monastic discipline, active participation of laymen in Buddhist life and the dual practice of Zen and Pure Land.

**Master Tsung-pen**, also known as I-yuan, was a sixteenth century Chinese Zen Master who lectured widely on the Buddhist Canon. Recognition was, in time, granted by the Emperor, who conferred upon him the title Master of Merit and Virtue. Elder Master Tsung-pen wrote the commentary excerpted in this volume while serving as abbot of the temple appropriately known as Pure-Land Zen Monastery.

# Other Books in the Pure Land series*

## Buddhism of Wisdom and Faith
### Pure Land Principles and Practice
(5th ed.: 1994)

## Horizontal Escape
### Pure Land Buddhism in Theory and Practice
(A special edition of *Buddhism of Wisdom and Faith*)
(1994)

## Pure-Land Zen/Zen Pure-Land
### Letters from Patriarch Yin Kuang
(2nd ed.: 1993)

## Pure Land of the Patriarchs
### Zen Master Han-Shan on Pure Land Buddhism
(1993)

## Pure Land Buddhism
### Dialogues with Ancient Masters
(3rd ed.: 1992)

*Available from the following sources:

Sutra Translation Committee of the
United States and Canada
2611 Davidson Avenue
Bronx, NY 10468 (USA). Tel. (718) 584-0621

International Buddhist Monastic Institute
9250 Columbus Avenue
North Hills, CA 91343 (USA). Tel. (818) 893-5317

Corporate Body of the Buddha
Educational Foundation
11th Floor, 55 Hang Chow S. Road Sec.1
Taipei, Taiwan. Tel. (02)3951198

# Contents

*Faith is the basis of the Path, the*
*mother of virtues,*
*Nourishing and growing all good ways,*
*Cutting away the net of doubt,*
*Freeing from the torrent of passion ...*
*Faith can assure arrival at enlightenment.*

*Avatamsaka Sutra*

# Publisher's Foreword

In what appears to be a long time ago, in the summer of 1990, a friend drew our attention to a manuscript anthologizing the teachings of two eminent Chinese masters of the sixteenth century. We recall reading through the text with keen interest, hoping that it would soon become widely available.

The matter then skipped our minds as we busied ourselves, in the intervening years, with editing and publishing the four-volume Pure Land Series of the Sutra Translation Committee. One thing leading to another, in early 1993, we were reminded of the manuscript, still unpublished at the time, and opened discussions in earnest with the translator, Dr. J.C. Cleary. One more year would go by, however, before the matter was finally settled, thanks in large part to the assistance of Master Lok To and Mr. Lee Tsu-ku.

Causes and conditions having finally met, we believe that the reader will find Dr. Cleary's translation a lucid and inspiring text on Pure Land -- a Buddhist tradition widely followed in Asia but little known in the West.

The present volume contains Dr. Cleary's original manuscript, except for the section on Master Chu-hung's "Answers to Forty-Eight Questions on the Pure Land," which is being considered for a separate publication. Transcription of names is in the Wade-Giles system to conform to other works in this Pure Land Series.

*** 

To those pressed for time and hungry for solace, Buddha Sakyamuni left behind a treasure trove of 84,000 Dharma gems. All of them are rare, exquisite and priceless, beyond mankind's deepest and wildest dreams. Whatever gem strikes your fancy, be it the brilliant Zen diamond or the fiery Esoteric ruby, do not forget the translucent green jade of *Pure Land*, bestowed upon Sudhana -- the quintessential seeker of the Way. In the words of the Bodhisattva Samantabhadra, Sudhana's fifty-third and last teacher in the *Avatamsaka Sutra*:

> *The supreme and endless blessings*
> *of Samantabhadra's deeds,*
> *I now universally transfer.*
> *May every living being, drowning*
> *and adrift,*
> *Soon return to the Land of Limitless*
> *Light -- of Amitabha Buddha!*

*D.Phung/Minh Thanh/P.D.Leigh*
*Rye Brook: Ullambana '94*

# Note on Pure Land

Of the various forms of Buddhism that developed after the demise of the historical Buddha in 480 B.C., Mahayana (the "Great Vehicle") became the dominant tradition in East and parts of Southeast Asia. This broad area encompasses China, Korea, Vietnam and Japan, among other countries.

In time, a number of schools arose within Mahayana Buddhism in accordance with the capacities and circumstances of the people, the main ones being the Zen, Pure Land and Esoteric schools. Among these schools, Pure Land has the greatest number of adherents, although its teachings and methodology are not widely known in the West.

Given its popular appeal, [Pure Land] quickly became the object of the most dominant form of Buddhist devotion in East Asia. (M. Eliade, ed., *Encyclopedia of Religions*, Vol. 12.)

## What is Pure Land?

[Pure Land comprises the schools] of East Asia which emphasize aspects of Mahayana Buddhism stressing faith in Amida, meditation on and recitation of his name, and the religious goal of being reborn in his "Pure Land," or "Western Paradise." (Crim, *Perennial Dictionary of World Religions.*)

The most common Pure Land practice is the recitation of Amitabha Buddha's name. This should be done with utmost faith and a sincere vow to achieve rebirth in the Pure Land.

Along with this popular form of Pure Land, there is a higher aspect, in which Amitabha, the Buddha of Infinite Light and Life, is equated with our Buddha Nature, infinitely bright and everlasting *(Self-Nature Amitabha, Mind-Only Pure Land).*

## Main Characteristics of Pure Land

i) Its teachings are based on *compassion*, on faith in the compassionate Vows of Amitabha Buddha to welcome and guide all sentient beings to His Pure Land;

ii) It is an *easy method*, in terms of both goal (rebirth in the Western Pure Land as a stepping-stone toward Buddhahood) and form of cultivation (can be practiced anywhere, any time with no special liturgy, accoutrements or guidance);

iii) It is a *panacea* for the diseases of the mind, unlike other methods or meditations which are directed to specific illnesses (e.g., meditation on the corpse is designed to sever lust, counting the breath is meant to rein in the wandering mind);

iv) It is a *democratic* method that empowers its adherents, freeing them from arcane metaphysics as well as dependence on teachers, gurus, roshis and other mediating authority figures.

For these reasons, since the thirteenth century, Pure Land has been the dominant tradition in East Asia, playing a crucial role in the democratization of Buddhism and the rise of the lay movement. Honen Shonin(1133-1212), the Patriarch of the Jodo (Pure Land) school in Japan, expressed the very essence of Pure Land teaching when he wrote:

There shall be no distinction, no regard to male or female, good or bad, exalted or lowly; none shall fail to be in his Land of Purity after having called, with complete faith, on Amida. (Quoted by Elizabeth ten Grotenhuis in Joji Okazaki, *Pure Land Buddhist Painting*, p. 14.)

# Introduction:
## Pure Land Buddhism

Buddhism has evolved many, many forms during its long history. Codes of conduct, guidelines for communal life, rituals, meditative practices, modes of teaching, images, fables and philosophies have varied greatly over time and place. According to the fundamental Buddhist principle of skill-in-means, this multiformity is natural and proper, a necessary response to the great variety of circumstances in which Buddhism has been propagated.

Skill-in-means requires that the presentation of the Buddhist Teaching, (sometimes simply called "the Dharma"), be adapted to the mentality and circumstances of the people being taught. According to Buddhist seers, the absolute truth is inconceivable and cannot be captured in any particular formulation. Therefore in Buddhism there is no fixed dogma, only provisional, partial expressions of the teaching, suited to the capabilities of the audience being addressed.

In keeping with this fundamental principle, a tolerant, nonsectarian approach has normally prevailed throughout Buddhist history. Where dogmatic controversies and sectarian partisanship have cropped up in the communities of Buddhist followers, these are distortions of the teaching, and have always been based on misunderstanding and misinformation. In embracing Pure Land Buddhism, therefore, people are not rejecting any of the other streams of the Buddhist tradition -- they have only decided that Pure Land methods are most appropriate and most effective for them.

*** 

Pure Land Buddhism is a religion of faith, of faith in Amitabha Buddha [and in one's capacity to achieve Buddhahood]. Amitabha Buddha presides over the Pure Land, a "paradise" in the west, the land of ultimate bliss, named "Peaceful Nurturing." In the Pure Land, there is none of the suffering and defilement and delusion that normally blocks people's efforts toward enlightenment here in our world (which the Buddhists named "Endurance.")

The immediate goal of Pure Land believers is to be reborn in Amitabha's Pure Land. There, in more favorable surroundings, in the presence of Amitabha, they will eventually attain complete enlightenment.

The essence of Pure Land practice thus consists of invoking the name of Amitabha Buddha, contemplating the qualities of Amitabha, visualizing Amitabha, and taking vows to be born in the Pure Land.

***

Making a vow to attain birth in the Pure Land signifies a fundamental reorientation of the believer's motivations and will. No longer is the purpose of life brute survival, or fulfillment of a social role, or the struggle to wrest some satisfaction from a frustrating, taxing environment. By vowing to be reborn in the Pure Land, believers shift their focus. The joys and sorrows of this world become incidental, inconsequential. The present life takes on value chiefly as an opportunity to concentrate one's awareness on Amitabha, and purify one's mind accordingly.

The hallmark of Pure Land Buddhism is reciting the buddha-name, invoking Amitabha Buddha by chanting his name. Through reciting the buddha-name, people focus their attention on Amitabha Buddha. This promotes mindfulness of buddha, otherwise known as *buddha-remembrance* [buddha recitation].

In what sense is buddha "remembered"? "Buddha" is the name for the one reality that underlies all forms of being, as well as an epithet for those who witness and express this reality. According to the Buddhist Teaching, all people possess an inherently enlightened true nature that is their real identity. By becoming mindful of buddha, therefore, people are just regaining their own real identity. They are remembering their own buddha-nature.

*Buddha* as such is a concept that transcends any particular embodiment, such as Shakyamuni Buddha (the historical buddha born in India), or Maitreya Buddha (the future buddha), or Vairocana Buddha (the cosmic buddha) or Amitabha Buddha (the buddha of the western paradise). Buddha exists in many forms, but all share the same "body of reality," the same *Dharmakaya*, which is formless, omnipresent, all-pervading, indescribable, infinite -- the everywhere-equal essence of all things, the one reality within-and-beyond all appearances.

Dharmakaya Buddha is utterly abstract and in fact inconceivable, so buddha takes on particular forms to communicate with living beings by coming within their range of perception. For most people, this is the only way that buddha can become comprehensible and of practical use. The particular embodiments of buddha, known as Nirmanakaya, are supreme examples of compassionate skill-in-means.

Pure Land people focus on buddha in the form of Amitabha, the buddha of infinite life and infinite light. Believers put their faith in Amitabha Buddha and recite his name, confident in the promises he has given to deliver all who invoke his name. All classes of people, whatever their other characteristics or shortcomings, are guaranteed rebirth in the Pure Land and ultimate salvation, if only they invoke Amitabha's name with singleminded concentration and sincere faith.

## Buddha-Name Recitation

Buddha-name recitation is practiced in many forms: silently or aloud, alone or in groups, by itself or combined with visualization of Amitabha or contemplation of the concept of buddha, or combined with the methods of Zen. The aim is to concentrate one's attention on Amitabha, and let all other thoughts die away. At first and all along, miscellaneous thoughts intrude, and the mind wanders. But with sustained effort, one's focus on the buddha-name becomes progressively more steady and clear. Mindfulness of buddha -- buddha-remembrance -- grows stronger and purer.

Reciting the buddha-name functions as a powerful antidote to those great enemies of clear awareness that Buddhists have traditionally labeled "oblivion" and "scattering." "Oblivion" refers to the tendency of the human mind when not occupied by its habitual thoughts to sink into a state of torpor and sleepy nescience. "Scattering" is the other pole of ordinary mental life, where the consciousness flies off in all directions pursuing objects of thought and desire.

Through the centuries, those who practice it have found that buddha-name recitation is a much more beneficial use of mind than the ordinary run of hopes and fears that would otherwise preoccupy their minds. Calm focus replaces agitation and anxiety, producing a most invigorating saving of energy. "Mixed mindfulness is the disease. Mindfulness of buddha is the medicine."

According to the Pure Land teaching, all sorts of evil karma are dissolved by reciting the buddha-name wholeheartedly and singlemindedly.[1] What is karma? In Buddhist terms, "karma" means "deeds," "actions." Through sequences of cause and effect, what we do and what those we interact with do determines our experience and shapes our perceptions, which in turn guides our further actions.

Habitual patterns of perception and behavior build up and acquire momentum. Now we are in the grips of "karmic consciousness," so-called because it is a state of mind at once the result of past deeds and the source of future deeds. This is the existential trap from which all forms of Buddhist practice aim to extricate us.

According to the Pure Land teaching, buddha-name recitation is more effective for this purpose than any other practice, and can be carried out by anyone. The key is being singleminded, focusing the mind totally on Amitabha, and thus interrupting the onward flow of karmic consciousness. This is where Zen and Pure Land meet.

## All Classes Go to the Pure Land

Buddha-name recitation enables all classes of people to attain birth in the Pure Land, from the most virtuous Buddhist saints, to those who are incapable of meritorious actions and do not develop the aspiration for enlightenment.

In Pure Land terminology, "nine classes" go to the Pure Land. The highest class are those who achieve the traditional goals of Buddhism -- that is, who free themselves from desire, observe the precepts, and practice the six perfections of giving, discipline, forbearance, energetic progress, meditation and wisdom. The lowest class who go to the Pure Land are those who keep on, as wayward human animals, piling up evil karma and committing all kinds of sins: even they can attain birth in the Pure Land, if only they focus their minds and recite the buddha-name.

Buddha-name recitation in itself dissolves away evil karma, no matter how serious – so say the Pure Land teachings. Infinity lies latent in the gaps within moment-to-moment mundanity – in the Zen formulation. But above all it is the power of Amitabha that makes birth in the Pure Land possible for sinners as well as saints, because Amitabha has vowed to save all who faithfully and singlemindedly invoke his name.[2]

## The Pure Land

Amitabha's Pure Land is depicted in a way designed to attract believers. In the Pure Land there is no sickness, old age, or death. The sufferings and difficulties of this world do not exist. Those born in the Pure Land come forth there from lotus flowers, not from a woman's womb in pain and blood, and once born they are received and welcome by Amitabha and his assistants. They receive immortal, transformed bodies, and are beyond the danger of falling back into lesser incarnations. They are in the direct presence of Amitabha Buddha and the great bodhisattvas Kuan-yin (Avalokitesvara) and Shih-chih (Mahasthamaprapta), who aid in their ultimate enlightenment.

Those who go to the Pure Land live there among beings of the highest virtue. Beautiful clothing and fine food are provided to them ready-made. There are no extremes of heat and cold. Correct states of concentration are easy to achieve and maintain. There are no such things as greed, ignorance, anger, strife, or laziness.

The Pure Land is described, metaphorically, as resplendent with all manner of jewels and precious things, towers of agate, palaces of jade. There are huge trees made of various gems, covered with fruits and flowers. Giant lotuses spread their fragrance everywhere. There are pools, also made of seven jewels, and filled with the purest water, which adjusts itself to the depth and temperature the bathers prefer. Underfoot, gold covers the ground. Flowers fall from the sky day and night, and the whole sky is covered with a net made of gold and silver and pearls. The Pure Land is perfumed with beautiful scents and filled with celestial music.

Most precious of all, in the Pure Land, we are told, not only the buddha and bodhisattvas, Amitabha and his assistants, but even the birds and the trees (as manifestations of Amitabha) are continuously expounding the Dharma, the Buddhist Teaching.[3]

## Pure Land Literature

Pure Land literature offers many stories presented as real-life biographical accounts which corroborate the efficacy of Pure Land practice, and the description of the Pure Land paradise drawn from the scriptures. Like most Buddhist biographies written in China, these accounts are very terse, and focus on the subject's religious life. There are stories of men and women, monks and nuns, nobles and high officials and commoners too, people young and old in various stations of life, all devoted to Pure Land practice.

The stories often relate people's early experience of Buddhism, and note the various practices they took up and the scriptures they studied. In due time, as the stories tell it, their faith in Pure Land is awakened, perhaps by meeting an inspirational teacher, perhaps through a dream or vision, perhaps from hearing the Pure Land scriptures, perhaps from personal acquaintance with a devoted Pure Land practitioner.

The stories always make a point of the zeal and dedication of the true believer in reciting the buddha-name. Here are some typical descriptions:

"He cut off his motivation for worldly things and dedicated his mind to the Pure Land."

"He concentrated his mind on reciting the buddha-name."

"She recited the buddha-name with complete sincerity."

"He set his will on the Pure Land."

"She recited the buddha-name day and night without stopping."

"He recited the buddha-name singlemindedly."

"She developed the mind of faith and recited the buddha-name tirelessly."

"She turned her mind to buddha-name recitation and practiced it wholeheartedly, never slacking off."

"The older he became, the more earnest he was in reciting the buddha-name."

This is the message of the Pure Land life stories.

The climax of a typical Pure Land biography comes in the subject's death scene, when buddha-name recitation is rewarded and the Pure Land teachings are confirmed.

The believer dies peacefully, even joyously, with mind and body composed, in full confidence of rebirth in paradise, reciting the buddha-name. Often the Pure Land devotee is able to predict his or her own death in advance, and calmly bid farewell to loved ones. Sometimes the believer receives reassuring visits from Amitabha in dreams or visions to prepare her or him to face the end.

Various signs give proof that the dying person is about to be reborn in the Pure Land. Uncanny fragrances and supernatural colored lights fill the room. Celestial music is heard. Flowers from the Pure Land appear: yellow lotuses, green lotuses, golden lotuses. The dying person sees Amitabha coming from the west to welcome him, or feels Amitabha's hand on his head, or sees Amitabha accompanied by Kuan-yin and Shih-chih appear to lead him to paradise. The dying person sees visions of the Pure Land: Amitabha and his companions seated on a jeweled dais, or the seven jewel ponds, or a staircase of gems leading up to the Pure Land.

Those close to the dying believer receive assurances that rebirth in the Pure Land is imminent. In the most frequent motif, the dying person announces to his or her companions, "Buddha is coming to welcome me!" The dying person's relatives dream of a lotus opening in the Pure Land's jewel pond, with their reborn kinsman appearing inside it. Or the relatives see visions of the deceased riding off to the west on a green lotus. Or the dead person visits the survivors in dreams and assures them that she has indeed been reborn in the Pure Land.

After the person dies, the people in the room perceive a magical fragrance and hear celestial music gradually fading away toward the west. A golden lotus might appear on the death bed or on top of the coffin. The dead believer's corpse does not decompose. Auspicious colored clouds hang over the funeral pyre.

With elements like these, the death scenes in Pure Land biographies are meant to prove to the faithful that rebirth in the Pure Land is indeed the guaranteed fate of those who recite the buddha-name.

\*\*\*

Besides collections of believers' biographies, Pure Land literature includes other types of works designed to promote faith in the Pure Land teachings.

Many commentaries were composed on the sutras basic to Pure Land Buddhism: the *Amitabha Sutra,* the *Contemplation of Amitabha Sutra (Meditation Sutra),* and the *Sutra of Infinite Life (Longer Amitabha Sutra).*

Pure Land adepts also wrote essays to explain Pure Land beliefs in terms of Great Vehicle Buddhism as a whole, and to answer objections to Pure Land teachings and clarify points of doubt.

Some writers linked the Pure Land teaching to the other currents in Buddhism by picking out references to Amitabha's Pure Land and buddha-name recitation contained in the Buddhist scriptures and philosophical treatises not identified with the Pure Land school.

There are many records of talks given by famous Pure Land teachers down through the centuries, and personal letters they wrote, urging people to adopt Pure Land

practice as the most effective way to make progress on the
Buddhist Path.

## Pure Land Associations

For many Pure Land Buddhists, an important means
of strengthening their faith has been membership in a
group of fellow believers. The faithful join to form Pure
Land associations, where they can meet regularly with
like-minded people to recite the buddha-name and, if they
are fortunate, listen to genuine teachers expound Pure
Land texts. Though buddha-name recitation can of course be
done alone in private, many people have found group recitation
very powerful in helping them to focus their attention. Being
part of a community with shared beliefs helps to reinforce the
dedication of the individual and his belief that Pure Land is a
correct application of the Dharma that really works for people
of that place and time. When methods are being applied
correctly, the group also provides the individual believer with
living examples of the mental strength and unshakable serenity
acquired by longterm practitioners of buddha-name recitation.

Pure Land adepts often founded teaching centers
where people could gather to recite the buddha-name and
hear the Pure Land doctrine. They enrolled believers in
religious associations dedicated to buddha-remembrance,
with their own bylaws for membership, scheduled
meetings, and guidelines for practice. Though many
monks and nuns practiced buddha-name recitation, and
many lay Buddhists pursued Pure Land practice on their
own, the typical institutional form of Pure Land

Buddhism was the voluntary association of laypeople, sometimes, but not always, led by monks and nuns.

On a purely social level, Pure Land associations could evolve into communities that offered their members not only ideological companionship and a sense of belonging, but also tangible material support in the form of mutual aid and a network of people who could be trusted and relied on. In many times and places, Pure Land societies have had their own facilities and funds. Under oppressive conditions, where the local social structure offered little security and much institutionalized violence and exploitation, popular religious groupings might become the real locus of loyalty and community feeling.

## Pure Land Buddhism as Other-worldly

Among the many varieties of Buddhism, the Pure Land teaching most deserves the epithet "other-worldly," often erroneously applied to Buddhism as a whole. Pure Land doctrine teaches that this world is an arena of unavoidable suffering and frustration, and holds out the vivid prospect of rebirth in another, better world, where sickness, pain and death do not exist. This world is a hopeless trap, from which we can escape only by the power of Amitabha. Unless we attain rebirth in the Pure Land, peace and happiness, to say nothing of enlightenment, are beyond reach ...

From a Buddhist perspective, it is the modern "this-worldly" orientation to life that is a form of unrealistic escapism and unwarranted pessimism about human possibilities. It is unrealistic because it seeks the meaning of life in gratifications that can only be temporary and partial: it seeks escape from mortality in transient pleasures. It is unnecessarily pessimistic because it ignores or denies the transcendental capacity inherent in humankind: "turning one's back on enlightenment to join with the dusts."

## Pure Land Buddhism within the Buddhist Spectrum

What was the relationship between Pure Land and the other forms of Buddhism in East Asia?

Pure Land teaching incorporated many of the standards and perspectives that were basic in popular Buddhism as a whole, deriving from the Buddhist scriptures. Pure Land teachers urged their listeners to observe the basic Buddhist moral code, to refrain from killing, stealing, lying, sexual excess, and intoxication. Strict vegetarianism was encouraged, as a corollary to the precept against taking life. Pure Land people were to give their allegiance to the "Three Jewels," that is, the enlightened one (Buddha), the teaching of enlightenment (Dharma), and the community of seekers (Sangha).

Pure Land teachers adopted the usual Buddhist moral perspective of cause and effect, of rewards and punishments according to one's actions. Pure Land people were taught to accumulate merit by good works, such as giving charity to the needy, helping widows and orphans, maintaining public facilities, supporting monks and nuns, contributing money and supplies for ceremonies and rituals, and making donations to Buddhist projects like building temples, casting statues and painting images, and copying and printing scriptures. Many Pure Land believers, in addition to reciting the buddha-name, studied and chanted various Buddhist scriptures, like the *Lotus Sutra*, the *Diamond Sutra*, and the *Flower Ornament (Avatamsaka) Sutra*. All these merit-making activities were viewed as auxiliary to the main work of reciting the buddha-name.

Pure Land theorists were faced with the task of clarifying their teaching of salvation through faith in Amitabha, given the mainstream scriptural Buddhist view of salvation as the reward for eons of diligent effort at self-discipline and purification and refinement of perceptions. By holding out the prospect of rebirth in the Pure Land through buddha-name recitation even to sinners, the Pure Land teaching appears to depart from a strict rule of karmic reward, which emphasizes the individual's own efforts as the decisive factor in spiritual attainment.

The Pure Land teachers explained this apparent anomaly by appealing to the infinite compassion of Amitabha Buddha (as an expedient embodiment of the infinitely pervasive Dharmakaya Buddha), who promises that all who invoke his name will attain birth in his Pure Land. The pioneers of the Pure Land teaching indeed took the position that for people in the later ages, the arduous path of self-restraint and purification proposed in the old Buddhist scriptures was no longer feasible. For average people, the only hope of salvation would be to rely on another power than their own, the power of Amitabha Buddha[4] [in addition to their own personal effort].

The Pure Land practice of reciting the buddha-name bears a family resemblance to the chanting of mantras that plays a major role in esoteric Buddhism. As the Pure Land master Chu-hung said, "Reciting the buddha-name is equivalent to upholding a mantra. After you have gained power by reciting the buddha-name, you will be able to face objects with equanimity." According to the Pure Land teaching, invoking the buddha-name brings into play the vows of Amitabha Buddha, whose supernatural powers bring those who invoke him rebirth in the Pure Land. The key element is faith in Amitabha, and the Pure Land teaching is propounded as an easy path open to everyone.

*** 

Reciting the buddha-name and chanting mantras can be seen to operate in similar ways, from the point of view of the analysis of the workings of the human mind taught by Yogacara Buddhism and adopted by the Zen school.

Both practices in effect suspend the operation of the discriminating intellect, the faculty of the internal dialogue through which people from moment to moment define and perpetuate their customary world of perception. As the Yogacara bodhisattvas pointed out, people ordinarily are not in touch with phenomena themselves, but rather with mental representations projected onto phenomena. What we ordinarily perceive is not the world itself, but a description of the world that we have been conditioned to accept. The internal dialogue of the intellect holds in place these representations, which make up the world of delusion.

By focusing on the sounds of the mantra or the syllables of the buddha-name invocation, the internal dialogue is stopped. Once its grip is loosened, the description it perpetuates is suspended. Then other descriptions of reality, other worlds, can come into view (such as Amitabha and the Pure Land, or the interplay of deities visualized in esoteric Buddhism, or the infinite vistas of the *Avatamsaka Sutra*).

\*\*\*

Operating in East Asia, Pure Land teachers had to reconcile their views with the perspective of Zen Buddhism. While Pure Land was the most widespread popular form of Buddhism in East Asia, Zen was the form that was intellectually preeminent.

According to the Zen school, since all people inherently possess buddha-nature, the potential for enlightenment, enlightenment equal to the buddhas can be attained in this lifetime by a properly directed and executed effort to break through the barriers of delusion. Rather than venerating the Buddhist scriptures as sacred but unattainable standards, the Zen people went to great lengths to apply the perceptions revealed in the sutras in practice. Generations of enlightened Zen adepts "appeared in the world" to demonstrate a freedom from worldly bonds and a mastery of the Buddha Dharma that proved that liberation was not an unattainable goal. Through their personal example and the unparalleled originality of their utterances, the Zen masters made a great impact on East Asian high culture in the realms of religion, philosophy, and aesthetics. The prestige of Zen was such that the other schools of Buddhists, and Confucians and Taoists as well, all had to answer to its perspectives.

***

The Pure Land school accepted the Zen perspective as valid in principle, but questioned how many people could get results by using Zen methods. Pure Land teachers granted that Zen might indeed be the "direct vehicle," but insisted that for most people it was too rigorous and demanding to be practicable. The Pure Land method of buddha-name recitation was offered as a simpler method by which average people could make progress toward enlightenment. The Pure Land teachers pointed out that many who scorned Pure Land methods as simplistic, and who proudly claimed allegiance to the Zen school, actually achieved nothing by stubbornly clinging to Zen methods. "With Zen, nine out of ten fail. With Pure Land, ten thousand out of ten thousand succeed."

The Zen school itself came to make room for Pure Land methods. From the time of Yung-ming Yen-shou in tenth century China, who was a master of scriptural Buddhism, Pure Land, and the Zen school, the synthesis of Zen and Pure Land figured prominently in the teachings of many Zen adepts.

In the Zen understanding of Pure Land, Amitabha Buddha represents the enlightened essence of our own true identity, while the Pure Land is the purity of our inherent buddha mind.     Buddha-name recitation is effective as a means to cut through the deluded stream of consciousness and focus the mind on its true nature. "Being born in the Pure Land" means reaching the state of mental purity where discriminating thought is unborn and immediate awareness is unimpeded.

The synthesis of Zen and Pure Land methods was epitomized by the "buddha-name recitation meditation case" taught by many Zen masters. "Meditation cases" (koans) in Zen are generally short sayings or question-answer pairs or dialogues or action-scenes which were designed for use as focal points in meditation. They were designed with multiple levels of meaning that interact with the mind of the person meditating to shift routine patterns of thought and open up deeper perceptions. Sustained concentration on the meditation point provides the opportunity for direct insights beyond the level of words.

Examples of meditation cases are:  "What was your original face before your father and mother were born?" "The myriad things return to one: what does the one return to?"   "What is the Dharmakaya? A flowering hedge."   "What is every-atom samadhi?   Water in the bucket, food in the bowl." Sayings like these were everyday fare in the Zen school. The Pure Land master Chu-hung whose teachings are translated below put together a detailed compendium of how to meditate with koans.

In the buddha-name recitation meditation case, the person intently reciting the buddha-name asks himself or herself, "Who is the one reciting the buddha-name?"

"Who is the one mindful of buddha?" The question is answered when the practitioner comes face to face with his or her own buddha-nature. The one mindful of buddha is the buddha within us. This is the Zen rationale for Pure Land practice.[5]

## The Present Translation

For this book I have translated texts from sixteenth century China that I hope will serve as an informative introduction to Pure Land Buddhist methods and teachings. The texts contain detailed explanations of Pure Land practice, vigorous encouragements to recite the buddha-name, and theoretical discussions relating Pure Land beliefs to the other branches of Buddhism. The synthesis of Pure Land Buddhism, Zen Buddhism, and the Buddhism of the Buddhist scriptures is very much in evidence.

These texts display the characteristic tone and concerns of Pure Land writings. They put forward the Pure Land teaching in clear language as an expression of skill-in-means, as the most appropriate and expedient method for people of ordinary capabilities to advance on the Buddhist Path.

After the rise of Pure Land Buddhism, many eminent teachers had occasion to explain Pure Land practice in terms of the all-encompassing theoretical outlook of Great Vehicle Buddhism as a whole. By the sixteenth century, late in the Ming dynasty, Chinese Buddhism was in a period of retrieving and reassembling its ancient heritage. There was a deliberate attempt by the learned to extract the gist of the classic teachings, and spread their message to a wider popular audience. Many Buddhist writers of the time offered reasoned explanations of the interrelationships among the various streams of the Buddhist teaching, harmonizing apparent divergences. Consequently, the Ming era Pure Land texts translated in this book are rich in information for modern day Buddhists of any denomination who are trying to comprehend the various parts of the Buddhist tradition in terms of the whole spectrum of Buddhist practice, thought, and imagery.

The works translated below serve as an overall theoretical and practical guide to the Pure Land teaching, placing it squarely within the wider tradition of East Asian Buddhism. As always, I have done my best to make the translation faithful to the substance and tone of the original, and in English as fluent as the original Chinese.

J. C. Cleary
Spring 1994

PURE LAND
TEACHINGS
OF
MASTER CHU-HUNG

# General Advice

## Remembering Buddha

The Pure Land teaching began with the World Honored One Shakyamuni Buddha, and has been disseminated through the generations of sage worthies.

They have divided the one gate of buddha-remembrance into four types: buddha-remembrance through reciting the name [of Amitabha Buddha], buddha-remembrance through contemplating the image [of Amitabha Buddha], buddha-remembrance through contemplating the concept [of Buddha], and reality-aspect (real mark) buddha-remembrance.

Though there are differences among the four types, ultimately they all go back to reality-aspect

buddha-remembrance. Moreover, the first three types can
be grouped as two: contemplating the concept, and
reciting the name. [Buddha-remembrance through]
contemplating the concept is explained in detail in the
*Sixteen Contemplations Sutra (Meditation Sutra)*. Here I
will discuss reciting the name. The Amitabha Sutra says:

> If a person recites the name of Amitabha Buddha
> singlemindedly for [a period of from] one or two up to
> seven days without allowing anything to confuse the
> mind, at the end of that person's life Amitabha Buddha
> and a multitude of holy ones will appear before him.
> As the person dies, his mind will not be deluded, and
> he will attain rebirth in Amitabha Buddha's land of
> ultimate bliss.

This is the great [scriptural] source from which for
myriad generations has come [the practice of]
buddha-remembrance by reciting the name, the wondrous
teaching personally communicated from the golden mouth
[of Buddha]. An ancient worthy said:

> As they contemplate the subtleties of the inner truth of
> phenomena, the minds of sentient beings are mixed
> [with other concerns than truth]. Since they practice
> contemplation with mixed minds, the contemplative
> state of mind is hard to achieve. The Great Sage
> [Buddha] took pity on them, and encouraged them to
> concentrate on the recitation of the buddha-name.
> Because it is easy to invoke the buddha-name, there
> starts to be some continuity [to their
> buddha-remembrance].

This teaches that the work of buddha-remembrance through reciting the name is most essential for being born in the Pure Land. If by reciting the name one arrives at the reality-aspect, then this has the same efficacy as subtle contemplation. Beings of the highest caliber must not doubt this.

All you children of Buddha here today, [I tell you this]: in the gate of repentance, everyone must repent -- even the sages of the vehicles of the disciples [sravakas] and the solitary [pratyeka] buddhas, even the great beings of complete mind [bodhisattvas], even those of enlightenment equal to the buddhas, all must still repent. Since they all must equally repent, don't they all have to be born in the Pure Land? How much the more so for those at the stage of ordinary mortals and those in the stages of study!

To all of you here today, disciples and others, whatever plane of existence you are in, I respectfully offer [this teaching] to you: all of you must wholeheartedly invoke the buddha-name, and seek birth in the Pure Land. I hope that Buddha's compassion will extend down specially to you, and gather you in and save you.


## A General Call to Remember Buddha

The *Amitabha Sutra* says:

> If people are mindful of buddha, at death they are sure to be born in the Pure Land.

The *Sixteen Contemplations Sutra (Meditation Sutra)* says:

> People in all categories who practice buddha-remembrance are born in the Pure Land.

Thus with this method of buddha-remembrance, it does not matter whether you are male or female or a monk or nun or layperson, it does not matter whether your social status is high or low, or whether you are virtuous or stupid. As long as the singleminded [remembrance of buddha] is not confused, all categories of people will go to the Pure Land, according to how much they practice [buddha-remembrance]. So we know that there is not one person in the world unworthy of buddha-remembrance.

If people are rich and high ranking, receiving the use of everything ready-made, they should practice buddha-remembrance.

If people are poor and destitute, with small families and few relations, they should practice buddha-remembrance.

If people have children to remember them at their clan shrines, they should practice buddha-remembrance.

If people are childless, and live alone on their own, they should practice buddha-remembrance.

If people's children are filial, so they are secure receiving their support, they should practice buddha-remembrance.

If people's children are rebellious, and feel no gratitude or love, they should practice buddha-remembrance.

If people are free from sickness, they should take advantage of their good health to practice buddha-remembrance.

If people are infirm, and closely pressed by impermanence, they should practice buddha-remembrance.

If people are old, and do not have much time left, they should practice buddha-remembrance.

If people are young in years, with spirit still pure and sharp, they should practice buddha-remembrance.

If people are at leisure, without cares to trouble their minds, they should practice buddha-remembrance.

If people are busy, and can only steal a little free time from the press of business, they should practice buddha-remembrance.

If people have left home [to become monks or nuns], and wander free of outside material considerations, they should practice buddha-remembrance.

If people are living as householders, then knowing that [worldly life is as impermanent as] a house on fire, they should practice buddha-remembrance.

If people are intelligent, and clearly understand the Pure Land, they should practice buddha-remembrance.

If people are stupid and dull, and can do nothing else, they should practice buddha-remembrance.

If people maintain discipline, the discipline which is the order of the Buddha, they should practice buddha-remembrance.

If people read the sutras, the sutras which are the words of the Buddha, they should practice buddha-remembrance.

If people study Zen, Zen which is the mind of the Buddha, they should practice buddha-remembrance.

If people awaken to the Path, the awakening that must be witnessed by the Buddha, they should practice buddha-remembrance.

I encourage all people everywhere as a matter of great urgency to practice buddha-remembrance. All categories of people will be born in the Pure Land: the [lotus] flower will open and they will see Buddha.

Seeing the Buddha, hearing the Dharma, in the end they will become enlightened. Only then will they know that their own inherent mind was all along fundamentally Buddha.

## Universal Encouragement to Buddha-Remembrance

Studying Buddhism is not a matter of adornments and formalistic practices: the only thing that is important is genuine cultivation of practice. Buddhist laypeople who live at home do not need to dress like monks and nuns. People who keep their hair can make a constant practice of buddha-remembrance: they do not need to abide by the daily schedules of monks and nuns.

People who like quiet can practice buddha-remembrance [alone] in silence: they do not have to form groups and create associations [for the purpose].

People who fear untoward events can practice buddha-remembrance [at home] behind closed doors: they do not have to go to temples to hear the scriptures.

People who know how to read can practice buddha-remembrance according to the scriptural teachings.

Burning incense [in temples] far and wide is not as good as sitting peacefully in a hall at home practicing buddha-remembrance.

Serving misguided teachers is not as good as being obedient and filial to one's parents and practicing buddha-remembrance.

Making widespread connections with deluded friends is not as good as preserving one's purity alone and practicing buddha-remembrance.

Storing up merit for future lives is not as good as creating merit in the present by practicing buddha-remembrance.

Making vows and promising expiation [of wrongdoings] is not as good as repenting past faults, undergoing self-renewal and practicing buddha-remembrance.

Studying non-Buddhist books and texts is not as good as being totally illiterate and practicing buddha-remembrance.

Engaging in false talk about the principles of Zen without knowledge is not as good as genuinely maintaining discipline and practicing buddha-remembrance.

Seeking demonic spiritual powers is not as good as having correct faith in cause and effect and practicing buddha-remembrance.

To express the essential point, an upright mind annihilates evil. If you practice buddha-remembrance like this, you are called a good person. If you practice buddha-remembrance while reining in the mind and eliminating scattering, you are called a worthy person. If you practice buddha-remembrance while enlightening your mind and cutting off delusion, you are called a sage.

I urge people who are completely at leisure to practice buddha-remembrance.   You have finished arranging marriages for your daughters. Your sons and grandsons are taking care of family business. You are secure and at leisure with no concerns. You should practice buddha-remembrance with your whole mind and your whole strength. Every day recite the buddha-name several thousand times, or even several tens of thousands of times.

I urge people who are half at leisure and half busy to practice buddha-remembrance. You are half through, half not through: sometimes you are busy, sometimes you are at leisure. Though you are not totally at leisure, when you are busy you should take care of business, and when you have free time, you should practice buddha-remembrance. Every day recite the buddha-name several hundred times, or several thousand times.

I urge people who are completely busy to practice buddha-remembrance. You are working on government affairs, or else running around taking care of family business. Though you have no free time, you still must steal a bit of free time amidst your busy life and practice buddha-remembrance. Every day recite the buddha-name ten times in the morning, and several hundred times during the day.


## Essentials for Reading the Sutras


What is explained in the sutras of the great canon is no more than discipline, concentration, and wisdom.

In reading the scriptures, there are two kinds of mistakes.

One mistake is to cling to the literal text and miss the inner principles.

The second mistake is to recognize the principles but not apply them to your own mind, so that you waste time and just make them into causes of entanglement.

If you can fully comprehend the practice of discipline, concentration, and wisdom, this in itself is what is called constantly abiding from moment to moment in the scriptural teachings of the great canon, and being mindful of thousands and millions of volumes of sutras.

We must also recognize that this discipline, concentration, and wisdom are equivalent to the method of buddha-remembrance. How so?

Discipline means preventing wrongdoing. If you can wholeheartedly practice buddha-remembrance, evil will not dare to enter -- this is discipline.

Concentration means eliminating the scattering [characteristic of ordinary mind]. If you wholeheartedly practice buddha-remembrance, mind does have any other object -- this is concentration.

Wisdom means clear perception. If you contemplate the sound of the buddha-name with each syllable distinct, and also contemplate that the one who is mindful and the one who is the object of this mindfulness are both unattainable -- this is wisdom.

Thus buddha-remembrance is discipline, concentration, and wisdom. What need is there to follow texts literally when reading the scriptures?

Time passes quickly, life does not remain solid forever.
I hope all of you will make the work of Pure Land
practice your urgent task. Do not think that what I say
is false and fail to heed it.


# A Talk to Householders


Human life: mothers and children, husbands and
wives. A person's family and dependents are all there due
to the nexus of causal factors from past lives.
Temporarily they join together, but in the end they must
be parted. This in itself is not sad or painful. What is sad
and painful is to pass a lifetime in vain, without being
mindful of buddha, without practicing
buddha-remembrance.

Today let us simply abandon the myriad
entanglements, turn the light around and reflect back.

Buddha-remembrance is the most important thing in
life. There not much more to say. Just be concerned with
purifying your mindfulness of buddha.

As you recite the buddha-name, reflect clearly in your
mind on every syllable. Be serious every moment: do not
let any false thoughts mix in. Every morning and evening
as you bow to the buddha-image, make a most earnest
vow to seek birth in the Pure Land.

If you persist in this [throughout your life] until you
are on the brink of death, correct mindfulness will appear
before you spontaneously, and you will go to be reborn

in Amitabha Buddha's Pure Land of Ultimate Bliss, reborn transformed in the Lotus Treasury World, forever removed from all suffering.


## To a Sick Person


The ancients had a saying:

> Sickness is the best medicine for sentient beings. When sick, a person should be very happy. When everything goes against your will, do not feel afflicted.

Another saying goes:

> Life and death are fated. When sick, a person should give rise to great liberation. Let life and death go on, without being afraid.


Again: The past is like an illusion. The present is like an illusion. The future is like an illusion. Abandon them utterly with all your feelings, and just uphold correct mindfulness. In the midst of your sickness, be peaceful and patient. Do not think restlessly of a quick cure. This is the best prescription for a fast recovery.

Also: Put aside all your household affairs. Abandon the myriad causes of entanglement. Empty your mind and be mindful of the buddha-name. Do not forget it for a minute, and your karmic barriers will dissolve by themselves. When your karmic barriers have dissolved, naturally you will sleep peacefully at night, and your body and mind will get healthy and strong.

The person practicing buddha-remembrance must vow to abandon this evil world, and be born in [Amitabha's Pure Land,] the land of bliss.

## To an Elderly Layperson

The body of form inevitably declines and weakens, but reality-nature never decays or perishes. Remove all entanglements, and purify and unify your mind. Pure mind, pure land -- this is how to achieve birth in the Pure Land, and spontaneously arrive at birthlessness.

## To a Good Woman on the Brink of Death

Although the bodies of men and women differ, their *luminous real nature* does not. Why talk of the five impurities [that afflict bodily life]? All that is important is the one mind. If you invoke Amitabha with your whole mind, you are sure to be reborn in the land of peace and bliss.

# The Esoteric Secret

## To Ta-t'ung

The ancients taught us to approach enlightened teachers, and seek spiritual friends, [that is], men and women of knowledge. But enlightened teachers do not have any means to transmit mind or impart secret methods: all they do for people is release sticking points and remove bonds. *This is the esoteric secret.*

Today we just recite the buddha-name with unified mindfulness without confusion. This formulation is the esoteric method for releasing sticking points and removing bonds. *This is the grand highway out of birth and death.*

Recite the buddha-name morning and night. Recite it when you are walking and when you are sitting. When your mindfulness [of Buddha] is continuous, then it spontaneously becomes a *samadhi*, that is, a stable state of concentration. Then you will not seek further elsewhere.

Also: The mind which has long been in confusion is hard to settle down all at once. If your mindfulness of buddha as you recite the buddha-name is not pure, do not worry. All you have to do is deepen your effort, reciting every syllable of the buddha-name clearly in your mind.

# Emptying Body and Mind

## To Wang Chih-ti

If your mind is empty, then your karma is emptied. If your body is empty, then your sickness is emptied. If

there is any doubt, you should wholeheartedly abandon
it.

The sutra says, "Whatever has form is empty falsity."
Belonging to the realm of empty falsity, [forms] are like
optical illusions, like bubbles on water, like things in a
dream. How can you think they exist [in any absolute
sense]?

Reduce your thoughts and worries, curb your
annoyance and anger, regulate your drinking and eating,
be careful in your conduct. Every hour, every
minute, simply make buddha-remembrance your
meditation topic.

Don't neglect it!

Then enlightened awareness will always be present,
and you will be fully awake and undimmed.


# Too Many Concerns

### To Ming Ta-hsiao

You have too many concerns that preoccupy your
mind too urgently. That's why you develop all these
illnesses.

Just work continuously [on buddha-remembrance]
without any breaks, without mixing in any other
thoughts. This is the work [for you]. Excessive
austerities are not needed.

False thoughts are powerful, but after a long struggle
they will submit. *Have no doubts about this.*

## Do Not Concern Yourself

To Wu Ta-chün

Do not concern yourself with whether or not you will become enlightened.

Do not concern yourself with existence and non-existence, with inside and outside and in-between.

Do not concern yourself with "stopping" [*shammata/samatha*] and "observing" [*vipashyana/vipasyana*].

Do not concern yourself with whether [this method of reciting the buddha-name] is the same or not the same as other Buddhist methods.

If the feeling of doubt does not arise, do not concern yourself with who it is or who it is not [who is reciting the buddha-name]. Simply go on reciting the buddha-name with unified mind and unified intent without a break, pure and unmixed.

## Mindfulness of Buddha is the Medicine

To Yu Kuang-hui

An ancient said:

Mixed mindfulness is the disease.    Mindfulness of buddha is the medicine.

When buddha-remembrance is correct, it cures mixed mindfulness. If you cannot cure it, it is because your mindfulness is not keen.

When miscellaneous thoughts arise, then use your mind to increase your effort to be mindful of buddha. When your spirit is unified and undivided on every syllable [of the buddha-name], miscellaneous thoughts will cease by themselves.


# Penetrate Through


To Wang Kuang-ti


Nothing is better than simply reciting the phrase "Amitabha Buddha." Recite it with your whole mind, with your whole strength, without any other thoughts at all.

This is equivalent to the [Zen method of contemplating] the meditation topic "No." You do not need to keep in mind "No" or any other meditation topic.

If you purify and unify your buddha-remembrance, and penetrate through in your recitation of the buddha-name, you will penetrate through in all places.

# The Place Where Buddhas are Chosen

To Kuang-ch'i

The Zen master Layman P'ang said in verse:

> From the ten directions we gather together
> Each and every one of us learns not-doing
> This is the place where buddhas are chosen
> Minds empty, having made the grade,
> we return home.

If you cannot yet empty your mind, for the time being diligently practice buddha-remembrance. When it becomes continuous from moment to moment without a stop, then your mind will spontaneously empty out.

# Why Are You So Afraid?

To Wu Kuang-shou

If you do not doubt birth and death, if you do not doubt the public cases [koans] of the ancient worthies, then why are you so afraid? Why has the arrow of anxiety entered your mind? Of this it is said, "The one who does not doubt still has doubts."

In olden times two monks had committed adultery and murder, but after a single word from [the enlightened layman] Vimalakirti, their wrongdoings were totally dissolved away.[6]

If you could be like those two monks right now, we would not have to talk about it. Since you are not this way, there is another method. The sutra says:

Reciting the buddha-name wholeheartedly once wipes away the serious sins of eight billion eons of birth and death.[7]

If you recite the buddha-name sincerely eighteen thousand times, all your sins will be wiped away. The evils which you have committed will then be like the clouds blown away by the wind, like the frost melted by the sun, like a drop of water thrown into the ocean, like a snowflake on a red-hot stove: cleansed away utterly and obliterated without a trace.

## To a Buddhist Layperson

Firmly uphold the five precepts,[8] and singlemindedly practice buddha-remembrance. Be filial and care for your parents, [to be sure,] but I still urge you to unify your mind and practice buddha-remembrance. Vow that both mother and son will be born together in the Pure Land. Pass your days according to circumstances. If people come with offerings, accept them, but do not go about soliciting donors. Do not form associations for buddha-remembrance. Keep to what's proper and cultivate practice. Then you will be a man of great goodness, a true Buddhist layman, in this age of the end of the Dharma (Dharma-Ending Age).

# Ambition

To Mr. Shih of Weng-men on Tung-t'ing Mountain,
who seeks to become an official in a future life

Though it may be good to be an official, if having
been an official, in a future life you fall from [that
position], you will experience measureless suffering.[9]
You must singlemindedly practice buddha-remembrance
and seek birth in the Pure Land. Even if you were to
ascend to the highest rank of officialdom, it is not as good
as ascending to the Lotus Treasury World among the nine
classes of beings [born in the Pure Land]. Practicing
buddha-remembrance and seeking birth in the Pure Land
is far, far superior to being an official.

# Being Near a True Buddha

To Mr. Shih of Xü-men on Tung-t'ing Mountain,
who seeks to become a monk in a future life

Though being a monk is good, if a monk does not
cultivate practice, in his future life he will fall from [that
position], and receive measureless suffering.[10]
You must singlemindedly practice buddha-
remembrance and seek birth in the Pure Land.
Being near false images of carved and decorated metal
and wood is not as good as being near the true Buddha
who is preaching the Dharma right now.

It is far, far better to be a monk in the Pure Land than to be a monk here is this world.


## To Students

These days many people like to talk about studying enlightenment and finally comprehending birth and death. They do not realize that in this world complete enlightenment is extremely difficult. They think of it as [direct, sudden] "vertical" transcendence of the Triple World [of desire, form, and formless states].

But even [someone who has overcome desire and reached the stage of] a "once-returner"[11] still has to go [to his death] and come back once more [through rebirth]: how much the more so, for an ordinary person! Most of the sentient beings in this world will have to be reborn in the West [in the Pure Land] first before they can be completely enlightened. The [Pure Land] gate to the West is called "horizontal" transcendence:[12] not one in ten thousand misses it.

# Warnings to the Assembly

## Plain Talk

After I left home, I went everywhere studying and paying visits [to teachers]. At the time Master Pien-jung's teaching center was flourishing, so I went to the capital to call on him.

[When I met him,] I got down on my knees and asked him again and again [to instruct me]. He said to me, "You should hold to your fundamental obligations. Don't go hankering after fame and pursuing profit. Don't go clinging to those you think will help you. Just be clear about cause and effect, and singlemindedly practice buddha-remembrance." I accepted his teaching and left.

My fellow travellers laughed at me, thinking, "Anyone could say these few sentences. You came from so far away, and this is all Pien-jung told you! Where's the loftiness, the subtlety? Actually [this advice] is not worth half a cent!"

I said, "This shows precisely what's good about him. We were thirsting [for knowledge], looking up to him, expecting to revere him, and so we came here from afar. But he did not trick us with talk of the primal source and subtle wonders. Instead, he just instructed us in the plainest, most sincere way with the close-at-hand, pure and genuine work that he himself has personally known. This is what's good about him."

From then on, up till now, I have in fact kept to [what Pien-jung taught me], and never abandoned it.

## Belief (Faith)

Of the essential gates for entering the Path, belief (faith) is number one.[13] Without belief, the essential things will not get accomplished, nor will anything good at all be accomplished.

Here is a worldly metaphor. When robbers are denounced and apprehended, the government always punishes them severely. If these robbers were let go and pardoned after their arrest, they would continue as before and not repent. Why? Because they would then believe that they did not have to pay back a cent for their nefarious conduct, and would get to keep for themselves profits beyond reckoning. Therefore they are made to suffer pain, so they will definitely not go back on their repentance.

These days people recite the buddha-name, but they are unwilling to get serious and really exert themselves at it. This is because they have not deeply pondered [the Buddhist Teaching] and come to believe in it truly.

I don't want to say that you do not believe in the Pure Land. [But remember], the World Honored One said, "Human life [may only last] from one breath to the next." The meaning of this sentence is not hard to understand. You have personally seen and heard [of the fragility of human life] with your eyes and ears, and you have experienced many examples of it. But right now when I demand that you believe in this statement, you are unable to do so. If you really and truly believed in this statement, I would not have to spend all my energy warning you a thousand times to practice the method of buddha-remembrance.

But [the natural course of impermanence] is like water flowing into a gully: no force can hold it back. The day before yesterday when we had a funeral for a dead monk, you saw an example [of the impermanence of life that Buddha was talking about], and you were sad and unhappy.

Let me warn you all and urge you on by telling you this: Today we hold a funeral for one monk, tomorrow a funeral for another. Before you know it, it will be your turn, and then it will be too late for regrets.

You must get busy with buddha-remembrance. Don't waste any time.

I see you saying to yourselves that time is precious, and saying to other people that time is precious; but when you are in the monks' hall chattering, you are talking and laughing and taking it easy as usual. In fact you do not [act as if you genuinely] believe that human life [can end] from one breath to the next.

## Gathering In The Mind

I see new students and young people who stick the word "Buddha" in their minds to block off worries and false thoughts -- which they then feel bubbling up even more -- and think that this is the work of buddha-remembrance. They cannot rein in their minds. They do not know that the root-source of birth and death over countless eons cannot be instantly cut off.

But the moment when myriad thoughts are flying around in confusion is precisely the time to do the work. The more you gather [your mind] in, the more it scatters. The more it scatters, the more you gather it in. After a long time the work becomes pure and ripe, and false thoughts naturally do not arise.

Still, [the very fact that] you are able to become aware that false thoughts are a serious matter, is due to this one word "Buddha." If you did not practice buddha-remembrance, false thoughts would surge on and on without stopping for an instant, but you would never manage to notice.

# Reciting the Buddha-Name to Rein in the Mind

In buddha-remembrance through reciting the buddha-name, there is reciting the buddha-name silently, there is reciting it in a loud voice, and there is diamond recitation.

When you recite it in a loud voice, it feels like too much exertion. When you recite it silently, it is easy to sink into a torpor. It is called diamond recitation when you recite it closely and continuously with the sound between your lips and teeth.

But do not cling to this as a fixed rule. If you feel you are expending too much effort, then go ahead and recite silently. If you feel you are sinking into a torpor, then go ahead and recite in a loud voice ...

Every repetition of the sound should come out of your mouth and enter your ears, and awaken your inherent mind. It's like a man fast asleep: another man calls, "Hey you!" and he immediately wakes up. This is why reciting the buddha-name is the best means for reining in the mind.

# The Death Toll

People today are unwilling to recite the buddha-name. They scorn the Western Paradise. They do not know that [the Pure Land teaching of] rebirth in the West is the expedient by which worthy sages of great merit and wisdom transform our mundane world [called] "Endurance" into the Pure Land [of Amitabha Buddha]. They do not know that, as a causal basis [for enlightenment], this [Pure Land method] is not for those of little ability.

Just look around at how many people die in this city in a day and a night. [For most of them,] it's not a question of birth in the Western Paradise: out of the hundreds and thousands [who die every twenty-four hours], scarcely one is reborn in heaven. Those among them who credit themselves with cultivating Buddhist practice accomplish nothing more than to avoid losing their human bodies [in their next incarnation].[14]

This is why our [Buddha], the World Honored One, with great compassion, taught this method [of buddha-remembrance]. [In showing us this method] his merit surpasses heaven and earth, and his benevolence goes beyond that of our parents. Even having our bones pulverized and our bodies broken to pieces would not be enough to repay Buddha's benevolence.

## Dying Well

When I was young, I did not yet know of buddha-remembrance. In a neighbor's house I happened to see an old woman who recited the buddha-name several thousand times every day. I asked her, "Why do you do this?" She said, "My late husband recited the buddha-name in days past, and [when he died] he departed very well. Therefore I recite the buddha-name like this. When my late husband departed, there was no sickness. He just invited people over and said goodbye."

[Given that laypeople can achieve such constancy in Pure Land practice], how can someone who has left home [to be a monk or nun] not recite the buddha-name?

# Letters

## Pure Land Zen

In the Zen school the most crucial work in developing enlightenment is keeping the attention on a meditation topic [koan]. People who practice Pure Land Buddhism take the buddha-name as their meditation topic [contemplating the question: "Who is the one reciting the buddha-name?"].

You will not be able to be in accord with these subtle methods if your mind is crude and your energy is unfocused. You must immerse yourself in reflecting back [on the meditation topic]: when your effort peaks and your momentum is exhausted, then there will be a message [communicating enlightenment] from the causal ground.

# Unborn Mind

Reply to Tung Hsün-yang Tsung-po of of Hu-chou

Mind is basically unborn: it is born when causal conditions come together. Mind basically does not die: it dies when causal conditions disperse. There seems to be birth and death, but fundamentally there is no going or coming.

If you can understand this, then you will be at peace through birth and death -- ever still, ever aware.

If you cannot yet [understand this], then you must wholly abandon your personal existence, and continuously recite the phrase "Amitabha Buddha," and seek birth in the Pure Land.

Even if the causal conditions [for your existence] have not yet ended, and your life is not yet over, reciting the buddha-name over and over is very beneficial. An ancient said:

The method of reciting the buddha-name is the eternal life of the golden immortals [Taoist deities].

# Who is Reciting the Buddha-Name?

Reply to Yü Ta-yen, Layman Yao-sun

To create faith in the Pure Land, you should concentrate on the basic [Amitabha] Sutra and its commentaries when you read the scriptures, and save the other sutras for afterwards. When you read the commentaries, do not read them through at one stint. It is better to read a little at a time and take many days to finish them. Savor them in detail, and you will deepen your faith in the Pure Land. The ancients said:

> Among the most essential methods of cultivating practice in the sea of birth and death, buddha-remembrance by reciting the buddha-name is number one.

These were not empty words.

Also: Since you have not benefited by recitation aloud, silent recitation, or diamond recitation, but on the contrary, have been injured by them, now you must lightly bring to mind the buddha-name, right when your false thoughts are flying around in confusion.

Once you can stay with this, then observe who it is who is reciting the buddha-name. Do this for a long time. As thoughts arise, observe: who is reciting the buddha-name? If thoughts do not arise, just go on observing [who is reciting the buddha-name?]. [As you continue observing], the work of keeping your attention on this, and the words themselves, will both cease, but this cessation will not hinder the work of keeping your attention on [who is reciting the buddha-name?].

# Contemplation

### Reply to Te-Ch'ing, Hsü Kuang-jung, Layman Huo-ju

You came asking about such matters as reining in the functioning of the mind, doing contemplation when sitting and when standing, and contemplating the concept and image [of buddha]. All these practices are carried out according to the occasion: there is no fixed routine.

But to contemplate impermanence all the time is not something that can be done by those who have not finished with sensory entanglements. Even though you cannot contemplate constantly, this is still [valid] meditative work [for you].

Amidst sensory entanglements, the method of contemplation is hard to perfect. It would be better when you have time off from your studies and from family business to silently recite the buddha-name. What's important is that every syllable be clear and distinct, that every repetition be intimately taken to heart. Then mind will rein itself in.

If you do this for a long time without giving up, stable concentration will be achieved: this is contemplation.

## Finding Lost Mind

Reply to Liu Kuang-shu, Layman Shou-fu, of Hu-kuang

Ordinary people have let their minds get lost. First they learn how to gather in their minds. Later they find their minds.

There is not just one method to gather in the mind. Buddha-remembrance through reciting the buddha-name is foremost among such methods in terms of being highly effective and easy to make progress in. An ancient said:

With the other methods of studying the Path, it's like an ant climbing a lofty mountain. With reciting the buddha-name and birth in the Pure Land, it's like [being in a boat] moving along with the current with wind in the sails.

When thoughts arise, it is not necessary to do anything else to annihilate them: just put your attention on the words "Amitabha Buddha" and keep it there with all your strength. This is the meditative work of gathering in mind. Suddenly you will awaken: this is called "finding mind."

## Fear of Death

Reply to Yuan Kuang-shou, Layman Hsin-yuan of Su-chou

The fear of death is due to not having awakened to fundamental birthlessness.

Fundamentally there is no birth, so how can there be death, and how can there be the fear of it?

But after all, it is not easy to awaken to birthlessness. Right now you must devote yourself sincerely to buddha-remembrance. If you recite the buddha-name for a long time until your mind is unified and undisturbed, then you are sure to awaken.

Even if you do not awaken, the power of a lifetime of reciting the buddha-name will give you the knowledge when you face death that you are sure to be reborn in the Pure Land after you die. It will be as if you have wandered in other towns, and then gotten to return to your old home. Amitabha Buddha will reach down to lead you into the Pure Land. Your joy will be boundless: how could there be any fear?

## Get to Work

### Reply to Layman Chang Shao-hsing

Arrange for a quiet room and cultivate Pure Land practice there together. This would be the best thing in the world. The room does not have to be very beautiful, just big enough for making offerings to Buddha, walking, sitting, and bowing.

And it is *not* necessary to wait till all the family business is done. Every day there are things to do: you may want to finish them all, but the day will definitely never come that they are all finished.

Get to work [on remembering buddha] right away -- you have already put it off too long!

In the sea of birth and death, the method of buddha-remembrance through reciting the buddha-name is the best.

You should devote yourself to it singlemindedly.

## The Sutras Never Lie

### Reply to Wu Kuang-ning, Layman Po-yang of Hsiu-ning

[You are bothered by the fact that] the *Surangama Sutra* distinguishes true and false, but never talks about such things as contemplating the Western Paradise [of Amitabha] and reciting the buddha-name.

Since this Sutra has no bearing on this, why do you create waves where there is no wind and say it is false? If you say the Sutra is false, then sitting meditation is false, maintaining discipline is false, lecturing on the scriptures is false, and even attaining enlightenment and entering nirvana are false.

What you should do is singlemindedly recite the buddha-name. Do not give rise to doubts [about the Sutra].

## Worldly and World-Transcending

Reply to Layman Sun Kuang-liang of T'ung-chou

You asked this question: "According to the world-transcending absolute truth, the worldly is identical to the world-transcending, so is it then unnecessary to seek transcendence? Since the true is not outside the false, what's the use of seeking the true?"

If you do not understand the idea here, then the best thing for you to do would be to singlemindedly recite the buddha-name. When your mindfulness of buddha peaks, you will awaken, and having awakened, there will be nothing to discuss.

Even if you do not have great awakening, you will still leave this world "Endurance" and be born in the Pure Land. This is transcending the world. Dissolving away mixed mindfulness and purifying correct mindfulness is the absolute truth.

For now do not concern yourself with transcending or not transcending, or with what's real and what's not. Just do the work [of buddha-remembrance] until your mind is unified: then naturally you will comprehend properly.

## Gaining Power

### Reply to Layman Wu Ta-ch'e

Reciting the buddha-name is equivalent to upholding a mantra. After you have gained power by reciting the buddha-name, you will face objects with equanimity. The first gate to liberation is feeling weary [with the mundane world] and becoming detached from it. But how can you handle what's before your eyes in order to get independent of it? If you keep on reciting the buddha-name for a long time, the time when you accord [with reality] will naturally arrive.

## Investigate Right Where You're Standing

### Reply to Chang Kuang-ching, Layman Hsing-yuan

No need to investigate the saying of Yün-men's that you asked about. He was speaking of [Zen, sometimes called] "the separate transmission outside the scriptural teachings." [Instead,] you should just contemplate this saying of Yün-men's:

You must turn back to what's beneath your own feet and investigate to see what truth it is.

This investigation will not be difficult, since you believe in reciting the buddha-name. Just observe who the one reciting the buddha-name is. This is investigating what's beneath your feet right where you're standing. Do this for a long time, and it will be as I said in *Correcting Errors*: no need to worry that you will not attain the ultimate, primal, most subtle thing.

## Luminous Awareness

### Reply to Layman Chin Kuang-chü

In your questions you spoke of "the final crucial barrier," "the most profound meaning," "accord with the fundamental ground," "directly pointing out this matter." Crucial, profound, fundamental, direct -- these are all important questions. But it is just a matter of considering what is close at hand. Apart from *this* luminous awareness blazing up, everything is unimportant, shallow, peripheral, circuitous.

This [luminous awareness] is where the mindfulness in buddha-remembrance arises. When you see through it, I guarantee that you will complete the great matter [of enlightenment].

After you read this, you must not start thinking and pondering and trying to figure it out, seeking comprehension through rationalizations. If you do this, you will lose it. Just investigate from moment to moment. When you have really accumulated power for a long time, you will spontaneously get it: only then will you witness enlightenment.


## Simple and Economical and Direct

To Sun Kuang-i, Layman Wu-kao of Chia-hsing


Let me add a brief note to your daily lessons.

Since at present you are still occupied with your studies for the official examinations, in your Pure Land work the important thing is to be simple and economical and direct. A lot of complications will not do. You do not have any spare time to recite Kuan-yin's vows or the *Diamond Sutra*, so just recite the buddha-name consistently. There is still quite a bit of merit in this.


## Medicine and Disease

To Chang Pai-hu Kuang-t'ien


False mindfulness is the disease. Mindfulness of buddha is the medicine.

A longterm sickness cannot be cured by a little bit of medicine. A great accumulation of falsity cannot be removed by a short period of mindfulness [of buddha]. The principle is the same [in both cases].

Don't worry about those false thoughts flying around in confusion: what's important is to recite the buddha-name intently. Every syllable should be clear and distinct, with every repetition following on the last.[15]

Maintain the recitation with your utmost strength: only then will you become qualified to go toward [the Pure Land]. Of this we say, "Truly accumulate power for a long time, and one morning you will empty out." It is like grinding down a pestle until it becomes a needle, like forging iron into steel. This is certainly no lie.

There are many gates for entering the Path, but this gate [of buddha-remembrance] is the quickest and most direct. You must not neglect it!

## Shortcut

### Reply to Wu Ta-chou, Layman Chi-li of Hui-chou

You do not need to worry about how deep your evil karma is or how dull your basic nature is. The sutra says:

A single perfectly sincere repetition of the name "Amitabha Buddha" obliterates the grave wrongdoings of eighty trillion eons of birth and death.[16]

Why worry that your [evil] karma is too deep?

An ancient sage also said:

There is a shortcut to cultivating practice: it is just reciting "Amitabha Buddha." Why worry that your basic nature is too dull?

When you see your friends, tell them this.

# A Moment of Mindfulness

### To Layman Liu Lo-yang of Su-chou

For a long time I have respectfully urged you to devote yourself to reciting the buddha-name and seeking birth in the Pure Land.

This Path is the most primal and the most subtle and wondrous. It is also the simplest. Because it is simple, those of high intelligence overlook it.

Birth and death are not apart from a single moment of mindfulness. Consequently, all the myriad worldly and world-transcending teachings and methods are not apart from a single moment of mindfulness.

Right now take this moment of mindfulness, and be mindful of buddha, remember buddha, recite the buddha-name. How close and cutting! What pure essential energy, so solid and real! If you see through where this mindfulness arises, this is the Amitabha of our inherent nature. This is the meaning of the patriarch coming from the West, [the meaning of Zen].

Even if you do not awaken, if you take advantage of the power of this mindfulness [of buddha], you will be reborn in the Land of Ultimate Bliss. Cutting off birth and death "horizontally" [by rebirth in Amitabha's Pure Land], not being subject to cyclical existence, in the end you will awaken to great enlightenment.[17]

My dear old man, I hope you will put aside the myriad things entangling you, and recite the buddha-name and keep your attention on buddha twenty-four hours a day. This is my hope for you.

## Where's the Reality?

To Layman P'eng Chün-chü of Chiang-yin

Few people live much past seventy -- how long can our lives possibly last? Now in this evening time [of your life], you better put aside all your worries and concerns, and see through this world. It's like a play. Where's the reality?

Just pass the time with the one sound: "Amitabha Buddha." Make the world of ultimate bliss in the west your own home. [Think to yourself]: "If I recite the buddha-name and practice buddha-remembrance now, later I will be born in the Western Paradise. How fortunate!" Generate great joy, and stop feeling vexed and afflicted.

If you encounter things that do not go as you wish, immediately push your mind to this one sound, the buddha-name, and quickly focus on reciting it. Turn the light around [onto the source of your own awareness] and reflect back. [Think to yourself:] "[In essence] I am an inhabitant of the world of Amitabha Buddha. Why then do I have the same views and consciousness as a worldly person, creating feelings of anger and joy one after another?"

Singlemindedly recite the buddha-name. This is the peaceful, blissful Dharma-gate of great liberation for people who live in wisdom.

# Break Through Delusion

To Chu Kuang-chen, Layman Hsi-tsung, of Chia-hsing

This is the way people are in the world. When they encounter pleasing situations, they feel happy and content. When they encounter situations that go against them, they feel worried and endangered.

Nevertheless, pleasing things should not be considered lucky, and adversity should not be considered unlucky. If you are sunk in things that your conceptual mind considers convenient, the intention of transcending the world will never arise. If you are sad and do not get what you aim for, then you will grow weary of the fetters of the world of physical existence, and therefore seek to transcend the world.

Thus, when the myriad sufferings extend before you, just contemplate them with correct wisdom.

[Ask yourself]: Where does suffering come from? It is born from physical existence. Where does physical existence come from? From karma. Where does karma come from? It is born from delusion. On the basis of delusion, you create karma. On the basis of karma, physical existence forms. On the basis of physical existence, you incur suffering. Just manage to break through delusion, and all of this is empty and still.

You may venture to ask, "What is the method for breaking through delusion?"

Just go to the fundamental meditation point and understand: Who is the one reciting the buddha-name? Who is the one mindful of buddha?

Take hold of your doubts over this, take hold and defeat them: then all delusion will be smashed. Think this over! Don't neglect it!


## Three Cures

I hear news that you are sick, so now I will explain three methods [to cure yourself].

The first is called "the cure by opposites."

Since your sickness comes from overwork and anxiety, you should use leisure to cure overwork, and relaxation to cure anxiety.

Leisure does not mean being lazy and indifferent. What I mean by "leisure" is doing away with all entanglements, and being like a newborn child, with the conceptual mind not operating.

Relaxation does not mean dissipation and lack of proper restraint. What I mean by "relaxation" is to know that the world of physical existence is like an illusion, like a dream; to go along with it according to circumstances, not being deceived by objects; and to abandon all your concerns about whether you will recover from your present illness or not, and whether you will live or die.

The second method is called "temperance."

Temperance is a matter of regulating what you drink and eat, and being careful with what medicines you take. Regulating what you drink and eat goes without saying. It is not right to take too many medicines. Some medicines may injure your stomach before they cure you, so that you cannot swallow any food, and there is a danger of ulcers.    You should discuss [any use of medicine] with an expert.

The third method is called "correct mindfulness."

This is what I talked to you about before:  suffering comes from physical existence, physical existence comes from karma, and so on.  Sickness is one form of suffering: the basis upon which it develops is the same.

You  must  work  carefully  and  continuously, investigating day and night [how suffering arises].

If you cannot find out, just put your attention on the question, *Who is the one reciting the buddha-name?* This is the basic koan, the fundamental meditation point in reciting the buddha-name.

Turn the light around and observe for yourself, until you know the ultimate locus of this mindfulness of buddha.   Then delusion will spontaneously break up. When delusion breaks up, that which develops from it is obliterated the same way.

You should work hard to carry out these three methods.


## Throw Everything into the Ocean

You must believe that everything is due to past causes. Throw everything into the ocean: not only favorable events and adversities, and your failures and successes, but even life and death.

Do not be worried or afraid.  Gather up your body and mind, turn your awareness around and reflect within on the fundamental meditation point: *Who is reciting the buddha-name?*    This is the most important thing to remember!

## Mindfulness to Cure Sickness

Mindfulness of buddha through reciting the buddha-name is not merely illuminating mind. It also cures all sicknesses. If there are people urging you to enter into Taoist magical arts, do not believe them. [If you do] I'm afraid you will lose your correct knowledge. I'm making a special point of telling you this in advance.

## No Time Left for Minor Matters

Your illness has reached the stage where it is very dangerous. You should take everything you want to say, write it all down in a letter, and send it to your sons and your mother, so that there are no concerns left in your breast, and you can singlemindedly practice correct mindfulness.[18]

If you had been able to believe fully in the method of reciting the buddha-name in the days gone by, then [by now] you would be able to reflect inwardly in the mind's eye on the buddha-name in perfect clarity without any interruption.

Then it would be alright even if you were to go today or tomorrow, or alright if you lived to be a hundred and twenty.

These are crucial words. We have been friends our whole lives. Now that you are at this point, you have no time left for any other minor matters. You should not long for life and fear death, and miss the great matter [of enlightenment].

## Since You are Sick

To Layman Wang Ta-cho

Since you are sick, you should take all your outside concerns, and your concerns for your body and physical health, and wholeheartedly abandon them -- make yourself totally empty.

If there is anything you cannot [completely] put aside, I urge you to put it aside for the time being, and deal with it later. When false thoughts blaze up uncontrollably, you must recite the buddha-name a few times and subdue them.

Worldly glory and wealth and rank are things that do not last more than a little while. Likewise, difficulties and pains are things that do not last more than a little while. Before long they are gone.

All sorts of things that happen are due to past causes. They are not things that our human power can do anything about. Wholeheartedly abandon them, and singlemindedly recite the buddha-name. I urge you to do this!

# To Illuminate Mind

To Layman Ch'in Ming-chung

There are countless gates to the Dharma: what's important is to illuminate mind. Of the essential gates for illuminating mind, none equals reciting the buddha-name.

When you have spare time from your reading and writing, or when your mind is troubled, sit quietly and recite the buddha-name. This is very beneficial.

When your mindfulness is on buddha, mixed mindfulness retreats and stops. With mind empty, objects are quiescent: what will you do with the subtle wonder?

I hope you will not neglect this by taking it too casually.

# Open Up the Darkness

To Ch'in Kuang-liang, Layman Jen-nan of Wu-chiang

The saying goes, "Open up the darkness, and release the karmic bonds."

If you understand, then the darkness is the light, and the karmic bonds are nothing but liberation.

If you do not understand, then constantly gather in the mind and recite the buddha-name. After a long time you will become quiet and steady, and you will spontaneously be able to generate wisdom.

# Pure Land and Zen Methods

To Wu Kuang-i, Layman Nien-tz'u of Nan-ch'eng

There are many ways to enter the Path, but for directness and simplicity, none matches reciting the buddha-name.

The method of buddha-remembrance through reciting the buddha-name brings salvation to those of the most excellent capacities, and reaches down to the most stupid and dull. In sum, it is the Path that reaches from high to low. Do not be shaken or confused by vulgar views [that Pure Land is only for those of lesser abilities].

Since ancient times, the venerable adepts [of the Zen school] have taught people to contemplate meditation topics [koans], to arouse the feeling of doubt, and thus proceed to great awakening. Some contemplate the word "No." Some contemplate "The myriad things return to one: what does the one return to?" The meditation topics are quite diverse, and there are quite enough of them.

Now I will try to compare [Zen and Pure Land methods].

Take for example [the koan] "The myriad things return to one: what does the one return to?" This is very similar to [the koan] "Who is the one reciting the buddha-name?" If you can break through at this "Who?" then you will not have to ask anyone else what the one returns to: you will spontaneously comprehend.

This was precisely what the ancients meant when they said that those who recite the buddha-name and wish to study Zen should not concentrate on any other meditation topic but this.

Recite the buddha-name several times, turn the light around and observe yourself: who is the one reciting the buddha-name? If you employ your mind like this, without forgetting, without any other help, after a long time you are sure to have insight.

If you cannot do this, it is also alright simply to recite the buddha-name. Keep your mindfulness from leaving buddha, and buddha from leaving your mindfulness. When your mindfulness [of buddha] peaks, your mind empties: you will get a response and link up with the Path, and buddha will appear before you. According to the inner pattern, it must be so.


## Repentance

To Wang Chih-ti, Tzu-ou Hsiao-lien of T'ai-ts'ang


Your family has practiced [Buddhism] for generations and is full of virtue. So why have you been afflicted with this severe illness? Can it be that there is no past karma to make it so? The origin of sickness usually comes from killing living beings. That's why I emphasize releasing living beings.

There is another thing I want to explain to you now. The merit of having a monk from outside perform rites of repentance for you is poles apart from the merit of doing repentance for yourself in your inner mind.[19]

Therefore I hope you will empty your mind, and put an end to all entangling circumstances. With your mind empty, concentrate your mindfulness on the sound "Amitabha Buddha."

As it is said, for buddha-remembrance through buddha-name recitation, it is not necessary to move the mouth and tongue. Just reflect back in silence with the mind's eye, so that each and every syllable [of the buddha-name] is distinct and clear, and the repetitions continue one after another. Go on from morning to evening and from evening to morning, from mind-moment to mind-moment without interruption. If you are in pain, be patient and endure it: pay singleminded attention to your recitation of the buddha-name. The Sutra says:

> One wholehearted invocation of the buddha-name wipes out the sins of eighty trillion eons of birth and death.

This is why the merit earned [by this] is poles apart [from hiring monks to perform rituals for you].

# Answers to Questions

## Before and After

### To Ku Kuang-yin

*Question*

The ancients already had [Zen], the direct pointing of the special transmission. Later they practiced Pure Land methods, wishing to be born in the Pure Land. Were the Pure Land practices created by vows after enlightenment? Or are [Zen and Pure Land] practices done together before enlightenment?

If they are cultivated together, this means a dishonest mind, a mind on a path that diverges [from the selflessness of enlightenment]: how could this meditation work be unified? If [Pure Land methods are used] after enlightenment, by that time all sensory realms are the Flower Treasury World, all places are the Lotus Land, everything is alright everywhere: so why would there be bliss only with birth in the Western Paradise?

*Answer*

True faith in the Pure Land and determination to be born there are not a matter of after enlightenment or before enlightenment. Though they make studying Zen their task, nothing prevents those who devote themselves to Zen, without managing to awaken, from making a vow to be born in the Pure Land. Because they cannot avoid being subject to future existence, and in the end will be born again, [for them to seek birth in the Pure Land] is not dishonest mind or mind on a divergent path.

As for those who have already awakened, an ancient said, "Do you imagine that with a single awakening you can equal the buddhas?" This is why Samantabhadra still makes vows, even as one of the protagonists of the *Avatamsaka Sutra*, for whom all sensory realms are the Flower Treasury World and all places are the Lotus Land. This is why even Samantabhadra will surely persevere, seeking birth in the Land of Peace and Bliss.

Since even those who are already awakened act like this, it is obviously also the way to act for those who are not yet awakened.

## Zen and Pure Land

*Question*

In studying Zen the important thing is "One mind unborn." In reciting the buddha-name the important thing is that pure mindfulness [of buddha] be continuous.

Investigating the method of reciting the buddha-name, the intent is for wondrous awakening and birth in the Pure Land. When reciting the buddha-name, mind and buddha are clear and distinct.

When studying Zen, both [mind and buddha] are cut off. Because they are cut off, the power of Zen meditation gradually prevails, and the power of buddha-name recitation gradually weakens. So then, later on, how can one achieve both [Zen] enlightenment and birth in the Pure Land?

*Answer*

"One mind unborn" *is* Zen; it's not "studying Zen." Heightening mindfulness and subduing doubts is called "studying." This is what the *Surangama Sutra* means with sayings like "Take this mind and investigate over and over again."

Both reciting the buddha-name and studying Zen involve mindfulness: there is no contradiction between them.

# Working with Mind

To Prefectural Governor Ch'ien Kuang-chan

*Question*

I have let this mind go for a long time already. Although I gather it in and try to hold it by reciting the buddha-name, I only can do this for a little while, and then I lose it again. How can I preserve [mindfulness of buddha]?

*Answer*

A land that has been in rebellion for a long time cannot be won back with a single battle. It is a matter of firmness and courage and not retreating. When the mind ground opens up to illumination, then naturally once [this state] is attained, it is attained forever.

*Question*

As soon as I put the chains on the monkey [of my restless mind], I gradually sink into a torpor. When I wake up and set it going again, it immediately scatters in confusion. How can I subdue it?

*Answer*

Stillness will cure scattering in confusion. When the scattering goes away, this gives rise to torpor. Wakefulness will cure torpor. When the torpor goes away, this gives rise to scattering. By maintaining both "stopping" [of false thoughts] and "observing" [the workings of mind], torpor and scattering both recede.

Right now you simply must recite the buddha-name with purity and illumination. Purity means reciting the buddha-name without any other thoughts. Illumination means reflecting back as you recite the buddha-name. Purity is "stopping." Illumination is "observing." Unify your mindfulness of buddha through buddha-name recitation, and stopping and observing are both present.

*Question*
[A sutra says:]

Seeking mind in the seven places, mind is not inside or outside or in between.

The Second Patriarch [of Zen] asked how to pacify mind [and when Bodhidharma told him to bring his mind forth, he had to admit] mind could not be found. [Bodhidharma then told him,] "I have pacified your mind."

This is not the realm of ordinary people. Now I want to abide face to face with this realm. How should I be mindful?

*Answer*

Don't be concerned with seven places or eight places or pacifying or not pacifying or face to face or not face to face. Just singlemindedly recite the buddha-name. A man of old said, "Go straight to supreme enlightenment without being concerned about any right or wrong."

*Question*

[A Buddhist maxim says that] taking care of one's life and making a living does not go against ultimate reality. The Buddha Dharma is dedicated to universal salvation, without regard for one's own skin, but [even though I try to practice Buddhism], my concern for taking care of my own life is still present to some degree. How can I reconcile this [apparent contradiction]?

*Answer*

If we go all the way to the *transcendent level*, not only do taking care of one's life and making a living not go against ultimate reality, but neither do killing and robbing and sexual excess and lying. If we talk in terms of the *worldly level*, to have some degree [of self-concern] is a constant principle of worldly life, and does not block the Path. But cheating and avarice are not permissible.

## Pressed by Suffering

To Layman Chu Hsi-tsung

*Question*
When pressed by suffering, how can we be mindful of buddha, how can we recite the buddha-name?

*Answer*
Confucius spoke of not going against humane standards even when hungry, hurried and upset. Though this work of not going against [necessary standards when hard-pressed] is not easy to perfect all at once, if you work at it without stopping, finally it will become spontaneous.

Likewise, if you practice buddha-name recitation for a long, long time, suddenly you will have insight. Then the Path will be present there right in the midst of suffering and joy, of adversity and ease. As the saying goes, "Coughing, spitting, shrugging the shoulders: none of it is not the meaning of Zen." It is just a matter of bringing it to full ripeness.

*Question*
[Is it true that] we [mere ordinary sentient beings] cannot achieve the contemplation of the special

characteristics of a buddha, which are so great and far-reaching?

*Answer*
The ancient worthies thought that since the minds of sentient beings are very mixed, it is hard for them to perfect the contemplation of the concept [of buddha, with all its inconceivable attributes].

[Consequently], the great sages took pity [on ordinary people], and urged them to devote themselves to reciting the buddha-name.

So now for the time being, you should recite the buddha-name, and put aside contemplation of the concept [of buddha], and not discuss it.

# Unifying the Mind

To Layman Chiang Kuang-hui

*Question*
[According to the Sutra, if one recites the buddha-name] with mind unified without confusion for one to seven days, one will be born in the Pure Land. What if mind is unified [in buddha-remembrance] for one to seven days, but after this one loses this unity again: can one still be born in the Pure Land or not?

*Answer*
After you have been able to unify mind [in buddha-remembrance], mind will be less scattered, and

will surely never again become totally scattered.

This can be compared to [the case of Confucius's favorite disciple,] Yen Hui, who went three months without offending against [the prime Confucian virtue of] humaneness. After these three months were over, one can hardly say that Yen Hui became an evil man [again, though there might have been slight transgressions thereafter].

Though falsity may spring up in the mind of the kind of person [who has unified his or her mind on buddha-remembrance for one to seven days], it will be like a speck of snow on a red-hot stove. Probably [if this happens] the merit [of that person's buddha-remembrance] was a bit thin to begin with.

## Everyday Practice

To Layman Wu Kuang-yin

*Question*

A person who cultivates practice maintains his efforts and makes it his duty [to do so] and solidifies his basic position. Suppose there is some carnal craving and weakness, but the person holds back and sits peacefully and reins in his mind and recites the buddha-name: can he still find the Path and be born in the Pure Land?

*Answer*

If he is truly able to unify his mind [on buddha-remembrance] and remain unmoved, then he can.

*Question*

[As I understand it,] what is important in reciting the buddha-name is continuous mindfulness [of buddha] from moment to moment. This much is certain. But there are times when one is not comporting oneself with formality of bearing, but instead seems disrespectful -- for example when one takes off one's headgear and loosens one's clothing, when one lies naked in the bath, or when one is relieving oneself. At such times should one recite the buddha-name or not?

*Answer*

Silent recitation of the buddha-name is alright at such times.

*Question*

Suppose there are two people. One eats meat but does not neglect to recite the buddha-name. One is a vegetarian but never recites the buddha-name. Which is better?

*Answer*

Both are defective. The one who recites the buddha-name is a little better, better than the one who does not know that buddha exists.

*Question*

In reciting the buddha-name [one can say] "Amitabha Buddha" or "Hail to Amitabha Buddha." There is a slight difference here: one version is fuller, one simpler. The text of the Sutra just speaks of reciting the buddha-name, which seems to indicate only the shorter form. But these days in the Buddhist community everyone follows the longer form. Ultimately, which is correct? Which form do you yourself use?

*Answer*
I use the shorter form when reciting to myself, and the longer form when reciting along with the assembly.

*Question*
One of your enlightening aphorisms is:

> Recite the buddha-name to the end of your days, and you are creating good fortune for the future.

But if our minds are focused on winning good fortune as we are creating good fortune, then they are not on the buddha-name. If we pick up one but let the other go, can this be called [reciting the buddha-name] with unified mind without confusion?

*Answer*
The clear mirror is originally empty. Things appear as they come, but this does not obstruct the mirror's emptiness.

When people only work for the future so that they will welcome it, and work for the past because they are stuck on it, these are sicknesses.

[For the following answers, the questions were not recorded.]

## Work on the Root

### Reply to Layman Chiang of Yü-yao

To cut off the root for living people is truly hard. If there is contemplation that is not pure, this means you are dealing with the superficial level. If you investigate back into where desirous thoughts arise, this is dealing with the root.

Right now you must investigate the one reciting the buddha-name. This is mindfulness of buddha by reciting the buddha-name. For now concentrate on reciting the name. You may contemplate buddha when you are bowing to the buddha-image.

## Unified Mind

### Reply to Layman Kung Kuang-ch'i

No matter whether monk or householder, people should hold to the recitation of the buddha-name, so that their minds are unified and unconfused.

Reciting "Amitabha Buddha" is the way to enter into [this state of mental focus]. If you recite just "Amitabha," do not be careless and look past it.

Reflecting back on *"Who is the person reciting the buddha-name?"* has the same intent as studying Zen.

You can read all the Great Vehicle scriptures, and then you'll see that they *all* view correct mindfulness as the paramount thing.

## Pure Land, Zen, and the Scriptures

### Reply to Ta-ching

You need not falsely seek the meaning of the scriptural teachings and the meaning of the Zen school. Just carefully recite the buddha-name. Recite it till your mind is unified and unconfused, and then you will naturally awaken.

## Prepare for the Future

### Reply to Layman Chiang

After the transformation of the body [in death], there will be more transformations of the body. You have not yet managed not to be subject to future existence, so it is important for you to seek birth in the Pure Land.

## Rebirth Transformed

### Reply to Kuang-ch'iao

An ancient said:

I would rather be among the lowest class living in the Pure Land, than be conceived again in the human world.

If you are tired of the troubles of physical incarnation, just carefully recite the buddha-name. If you singlemindedly recite the buddha-name, you will be born transformed in a lotus flower [in the Pure Land].

# Singleminded

Replies to an unknown questioner

*Question*
When one singlemindedly invokes the buddha-name, if one is also attached to seeking birth in the Pure Land, doesn't this verge on having one's attention divided?

*Answer*
Seeking birth in the Pure Land should be done when you make your vows in the morning and the evening. When you are invoking the buddha-name, be singleminded and unify your attention. You must not harbor [any other thoughts] mixed in.

The situation is comparable to someone studying for the examinations. Reading texts and writing essays is his work. What is the reason he reads texts and writes essays? He wants to pass the examinations and become a degree-holder. This is what he hopes for.

# Practical Advice

Replies to unknown questions by unknown questioners

If you sit upright to recite the buddha-name, I'm afraid your mind will be hard to gather in. It would be better to walk around [while you recite the buddha-name].

To come to grips with [the meditation case] *"Who is the one reciting the buddha-name?"* you must have true doubt arise.[20] If true doubt does not arise, just go on silently reciting the buddha-name for awhile.

Though the power of his vows [to be born in the Pure Land] may not be deep, a man who has stable meditative concentration [as in Zen] can still go to the Pure Land.

But for someone who cultivates Pure Land practice, then faith, vows, and practice are like the three legs of a tripod: it will not do if one is lacking.[21]

[At the end of the Dharma-Ending Age], whenever a single blade of grass is raised, it immediately becomes a spearpoint that can kill people.[22]

In this period all forms of the Dharma have already perished: all that is left for people's salvation is the phrase "Amitabha Buddha." If a person is able to have complete mindfulness of this phrase, then he can be a teacher to the world.

## Everyone Must Cultivate the Pure Land

The Pure Land Master T'ien-ju said this:

These days followers of Zen look down upon those who cultivate Pure Land practices as ignorant men and women. But in so doing they are not [as they think, only] looking down on [so-called] "ignorant men and women." Rather, they are looking down on [the great bodhisattvas] Manjushri and Samantabhadra, and [the bodhisattva-philosophers] Ashvaghosha and Nagarjuna [who all advocated Pure Land methods].

What an incisive comment! For those who still do not believe this, I give some references, so that they may have proof that this is not false.

In the Sutra *Contemplating the Samadhi of Buddha*, a verse of Manjushri Bodhisattva says:

I vow that when my life is ending, I will remove all barriers, see Amitabha Buddha face to face, and go to be born in the land of peace and bliss.

In the *Flower Ornament (Avatamsaka) Sutra's* chapter on vows, the verse of Samantabhadra Bodhisattva says:

I vow that when I am about to die, I will remove all barriers, and see Amitabha Buddha face to face, and go to be born in the land of peace and bliss.

In the Treatise *Awakening of Faith*, Ashvaghosha Bodhisattva taught that the most excellent method is to concentrate on reciting the buddha-name, and thus achieve birth in the Pure Land, from which there is never any regression.

In the *Lankavatara Sutra*, Buddha tells Great Wisdom:

The bhikshu Great Virtue, here called Nagarjuna, having attained the first stage [of bodhisattvas, called] "Joy," will be born in the land of peace and bliss.

Here I have briefly cited four great bodhisattvas. Other cases of bodhisattvas cultivating the Pure Land are too numerous to record.

[The founder of Pure Land Buddhism in China,] Dharma Master Hui-yuan of Lu-shan, awakened to the profound meaning of great transcendent wisdom, and was called the bodhisattva who protects the Dharma in the East. He recited the buddha-name and viewed the buddha-image and went to be born in the Pure Land.

The great teacher Chih-i of T'ien-t'ai subtly awakened to the *Lotus Sutra*. He taught contemplation, and became the grand ancestral teacher of the [T'ien-t'ai] school for myriad generations. He faced the West, elucidated the ten kinds of doubts [about the Pure Land],[23] wrote a commentary on the sixteen contemplations [of Amitabha Buddha], and fully discussed the Pure Land.

The great [Zen] teacher Pai-chang, who was the legitimate heir to whom [Zen master] Ma-tsu transmitted the Path, and whom all the Zen communities in China take as their source, prayed for sick monks and held funerals for dead monks so that they might return to the Pure Land.

The national teacher Ch'ing-liang, who succeeded to the position of patriarch of the Huayen school, and who was acclaimed as an incarnation of Manjushri, taught that Amitabha is [a form of the universal illuminator buddha] Vairochana. He also wrote a commentary on the *Contemplation of Amitabha Sutra (Meditation Sutra)*, and propagated Pure Land techniques widely.

Zen teacher Yen-shou of Yung-ming attained unobstructed eloquence [as seen in his encyclopedic masterpiece the *Source Mirror*]. He was a pillar of the Zen school and practiced the [Zen master Lin-chi's meditation plan of] the "four choices." He always extolled the Pure Land and was born there among the highest class.

Zen teacher Ssu-hsin Hsin was the successor to Huang-lung when the influence of his school was in full flourish. Yet he was very keen on Pure Land practice and wrote a text urging people to recite the buddha-name, to enable them to arouse their faith.

Zen teacher Chen-hsieh Liao succeeded Master Ch'un of Tan-hsia in the Ts'ao-tung school. When he became very well known, he came out of seclusion to help restore [the school, which was in] decline. He concentrated on the Pure Land, and wrote a Pure Land collection that circulated widely in the world.

Zen master Tz'u-shou Shen synthesized the five teachings in a verse in [his work] *Stories of Virtuous Women of the Great Land*. He said that the quickest and most direct method of cultivating practice is Pure Land. He established a Pure Land teaching center and earnestly encouraged his congregation [to recite the buddha-name].

Zen master Yuan-chao Pen continued the Path of T'ien-i and extended the school of Hsueh-tou. The thunder of his teaching shook the earth, and he was teacher and model to two dynasties. He practiced Pure Land along with Zen.

Zen master Chung-feng Pen got the Dharma from old man Kao-feng. His students looked up to him as the [Zen school's] central figure of the age. He said:

Zen is Pure Land Zen. Pure Land is Zen Pure Land.

Chung-feng composed a set of a hundred poems called *Thoughts of the Pure Land* to encourage people to recite the buddha-name.

The foregoing are ten venerable adepts [of Zen who advocated Pure Land practice]. Other Zen adepts and Dharma Masters and Vinaya Masters who cultivated the Pure Land are too numerous to record.

The *Amitabha Sutra*, the *Sutra of Infinite Life (Longer Amitabha Sutra)*, the *Sixteen Contemplations Sutra (Meditation Sutra)*, the *Drum Voice King Sutra*, Vasubhandu's *Treatise on Birth in the Pure Land*: these are sutras and treatises that concentrate on expounding the Pure Land. Other sutras and treatises that contain some mention of the Pure Land are too numerous to note ...

I hope you will investigate each and every one of these people, read their words, and consider their ideas. I hope this will put an end to your doubts and give you a decisive intention [to recite the buddha-name]. This would be most fortunate!

## Considering Suffering as Happiness

The flies in the privy are suffering exceedingly, from the point of view of dogs and sheep, but the flies do not recognize this as suffering, and think of it as happiness.

The dogs and sheep out in the open are suffering exceedingly, from the point of view of human beings, but the dogs and sheep do not recognize this as suffering, and think of it as happiness.

The human beings in the world are suffering exceedingly, from the point of view of the devas in heaven, but they do not recognize this as suffering, and think of it as happiness.

If we push our reasoning far enough, it is also like this for the devas in regard to suffering and happiness.

If we realize this, not even ten thousand oxen can pull us back from seeking birth in the Pure Land.

## Reciting the Buddha-Name Mindfully

Those of the world's people who have a bit of innate intelligence look down on reciting the buddha-name as a device for [those ignorant of the Dharma]. They just see ignorant men and women reciting the buddha-name with their mouths, while their minds are miles away. They do not know that such people are said to be [merely] repeating the buddha-name [verbally], not reciting it mindfully.

*Reciting the buddha-name proceeds from the mind.* The mind remembers [buddha] and does not forget. That's why it is called buddha-remembrance, or reciting the buddha-name mindfully.

Let us take a Confucian parallel. True Confucians think back to Confucius every moment: if they depart from Confucius, are they not still close to him?

These days some people are thinking of the five desires every moment, and they do not consider this wrong:

instead, they think mindfulness of buddha is wrong. Alas!
It is better to be ignorant than to waste a lifetime like
this. What a pity that intelligent people can do this --
others may be ignorant, but they cannot [delude
themselves like this].

# Repentance

There was a man carrying out the Pure Land method
of repentance [by doing prostrations].

A monk said to him, "Doesn't it say in the scriptures
that if you want to repent, sit upright and be mindful of
reality? How can you be so naive, with this repeated
bowing?"

The man asked, "What is reality?"

The monk said, "When the mind does not create
falsity, this is reality."

The man then asked, "What is mind? What is falsity?
What can control the mind?"

The monk had no reply.

The man who had been doing the repentance ritual
said, "I have heard that in repentance, inner truth is the
main thing, and particular practices are aids. Even if one
is mindful of reality, if actions of body, mind, and mouth
are very carefully controlled, it does not interfere.

"What's the reason? People at the elementary stage of
practice are not yet able to accord with reality itself, and

must depend on other causal factors to aid them. In the *Lotus Sutra* [Buddha Shakyamuni] says:

> I use other skillful means to help reveal the supreme truth.

"The *Awakening of Faith Treatise* says:

> If sentient beings in the age of the End of the Dharma are to practice this Dharma, there is the fear they will not always encounter an enlightened being [to instruct them]. The Tathagata, the World Honored One, had a different method [for them]: he taught them to be mindful of the buddha by reciting the buddha-name and to seek birth in the Pure Land.

"Thus we know that Dharma Master Tz'u-yün's method of Pure Land repentance [by doing prostrations] has set the standard for ancient and modern, and is most refined and effective on an intimate level. It is equipped with both inner truth and phenomenal expression, like all the glorious forms of repentance in the *Lotus Sutra*. Both humans and devas join to honor it. It is a great precious lamp in the dark street of the Last Age of the Dharma.

"[Tell me, your reverence,] did Buddha not say that making a living and working do not go against reality?"

The monk said, "That's right."

The man said, "If so, then [do you mean to say] that practicing repentance through making prostrations is not as good a making a living [in this respect]?"

Again the monk had no reply.

## Studying Zen and Reciting the Buddha-Name

In the first two reign-periods of the present dynasty, Hung-wu [1368-1403] and Yung-lo [1403-1424], there were three great Zen masters: K'ung-ku, T'ien-ch'i, and Tu-feng.

In regard to reciting the buddha-name, Tien-ch'i and Tu-feng taught people to contemplate [the koan] "Who is the one reciting the buddha-name?" K'ung-ku told people to just keep reciting the buddha-name and they would have a gateway to enlightenment. T'ien-ch'i and Tu-feng taught according to what was appropriate for the situation and the mentality of the times, and both were right. K'ung-ku spoke of simply reciting the buddha-name, and sanctioned that, but he did not say that studying Zen is wrong.

I have already explained this briefly in my commentaries, but there are still some people with doubts. They think that in studying Zen the main thing is seeing reality-nature, whereas in simply reciting the buddha-name, what is important is birth in the Pure Land. So they want to reject studying Zen and specialize in reciting the buddha-name. They say that the sutras only speak of reciting the buddha-name, and say nothing about studying Zen.

This theory is quite reasonable, and those who practice accordingly will surely be born in the Pure Land. But to keep Pure Land practice and reject Zen will not do. This is because a person who recites the buddha-name and [through studying Zen] sees reality-nature, is born among the top class in the Pure Land: how can he worry that he will not be born there? Therefore in my commentaries I preserve both [Pure Land and Zen perspectives] for people to choose from. Please have no doubts about this.

But if people take this word "Who?" and use it to depress their energy, and think that this is investigating the one reciting the buddha-name, they are very much misguided and mistaken, and they will commit a great wrong.

## Reciting the Buddha-Name Does Not Obstruct Studying Zen

The ancients said that studying Zen does not obstruct reciting the buddha-name and that reciting the buddha-name does not obstruct studying Zen. But they also said that one cannot study both. Nevertheless, there have been those who combined Zen and Pure Land, like Yuan-chao Pen, Chen-hsieh Liao, Yung-ming Yen-shou, Huang-lung Hsin, Tz'u-shou Shen, and others. These were all great craftsmen of the Zen school who kept in mind the Pure Land without obstructing their Zen.

Thus we know that nothing prevents people who study Zen and who investigate inherent mind moment to moment from taking vows to be born in the Land of Ultimate Bliss when their lives here are over.

Why is this? Though one may have an awakening by studying Zen, if one is as yet unable to abide in the eternal quiescent light like the buddhas, and is still not free of subsequent existence like the arhats, then when this physical body is used up, one is sure to be reborn. How can being born in the human world and approaching enlightened teachers here be as good as being born in a lotus flower [of the Pure Land] and being near to Amitabha?

Therefore, not only does reciting the buddha-name not obstruct studying Zen, in reality it is beneficial for studying Zen.

## Great Filial Piety that Transcends the World

Filial piety means children serving and supporting their parents [emotionally and materially] and making them secure. Great filial piety means establishing one's resolve to carry out the Path [of enlightenment] and make it manifest. The greatest filial piety is to urge [one's parents to practice] the method of reciting the buddha-name, and enable them to be born in the Pure Land.

I was born late [in my parents' lives]. I had just heard of the Buddha Dharma when the grief of their passing was upon me, and I was left with the extreme pain that lasts till the end of one's days, [the pain of losing one's parents when young]. I wanted to do something to help them, but there was no way.

I respectfully tell this to all of you. If your parents are still [alive] at home, do not wait too long to encourage them to recite the buddha-name. If your parents are dead, recite the buddha-name [on their behalf] for three years, or if this is impossible, for a solid year, or else for forty-nine days.[24] Any [of these options] will do. Filial children who wish to repay the benevolence of their parents' efforts should know this.

## Enlightened People Should Go to the Pure Land

Some people ask this question: "I cultivate Pure Land practice, but the Zen people say, 'Just awaken to your own inherent buddha, and you are finished. What need is there to seek outside for some other buddha and vow to be born in the Pure Land?' What about this idea?"

[Answer:] I think that [what the Zen people say] is really the highest form of instruction, but if you hold to it rigidly, you can go wrong.

Let me explain with a comparison. Suppose there was a person of outstanding enlightenment, the same as Yen Hui [the best disciple of Confucius]. Suppose further that a hundred miles away there was a sage like Confucius expounding the Path, surrounded by seventy philosophers and three thousand worthy followers. Would there not surely be some extra advantage for the person of outstanding enlightenment, having heard of their renown, to go and see them? Would it be proper for him to be smug about his own enlightenment and refuse to go see [the sage and his worthy entourage]?

Even if you have gotten some measure of awakening, if you do not vow to go to the Pure Land, I guarantee that you are not yet [fully] enlightened. As [Master] Tien-ju said [in a similar case]:

> You are not yet enlightened. If you were enlightened,
> no force no matter how great could pull you back from
> being born in the Pure Land.

How profound these words are!

## One Cannot Deny that the Pure Land Exists

Some people say that the Pure Land is nothing but mind, that there is no Pure Land of Ultimate Bliss beyond the trillions of worlds of the cosmos. This talk of mind-only has its source in the words of the sutras, and is true, not false. But those who quote it in this sense are misunderstanding its meaning.

Mind equals objects: there are no objects beyond mind. Objects equal mind: there is no mind beyond objects. Since objects are wholly mind, why must we cling to mind and dismiss objects? Those who dismiss objects when they talk of mind have not comprehended mind.

Some people also say that the Pure Land which is seen at the moment of death is entirely in the dying person's own mind, so there is no Pure Land.

[People with this opinion] fail to consider this. It would be right to say this is the dying person's own mind if he alone saw that which is seen at the moment of death by those who recite the buddha-name and are born in the Pure Land: the Pure Land, along with the congregation of saints coming to greet him, the heavenly music, unearthly perfume, the banners and towers and the rest of

it. But everyone there at the time [of the death] sees it:
they hear the heavenly music fading away toward the
West, and the room fills with unearthly perfume which
does not dissipate for several days. Since the heavenly
music does not proceed toward any other direction, but
toward the west, and after the person is dead, the perfume
remains, can it be said that there is no Pure Land? ...

Let me ask [the person who thinks Pure Land is
mind-only], "When hell appears to you at the moment of
death, is this not mind?" "It is mind." "Does the person
fall into hell?" "Yes, he falls into hell." [I would say]
"Then it is obvious that since the person falls into hell,
hell exists. Is it then only the Pure Land that does not
exist? When the mind manifests hell, the person falls into
a hell that really exists. When the mind manifests the
Pure Land, isn't the person born in a Pure Land that
really exists?" [As the saying goes]:

> Better you should speak of existence on the scale of the
> polar mountain, than speak of nonexistence to the
> extent of a mustard seed.

Don't do it!

## Pure Land Wherever You Are

Some say, "It's not that I don't believe in the Pure
Land, nor do I denigrate going to the Pure Land. But
where I go is different from other people. If there is a
buddha in the east, I go to the east. If there is a buddha
in the west, I go to the west. I'll go in any direction,

north, south, east, west, up or down, to heaven or to hell:
as long as there is a buddha there, I'll go there. I am not
like [Chih-i of] T'ien-t'ai, [Yen-shou of] Yung-ming, and
the others who sought the Pure Land exclusively in the
Land of Ultimate Bliss in the West."

These words are very lofty, their meaning is very
profound, their truth is very abstruse, but they cannot be
taken as a standard that can be followed. The sutra gives
a metaphor: "Those whose wings are weak can only stick
close to the branch." Thus we know that only those
whose wings are fully formed, whose bodies are strong
and whose energy is high, can soar beyond the skies, and
fly across all points of the compass. This is not
something that those who have first developed the
aspiration for enlightenment are capable of.

When the World Honored One taught Vaideshi the
method of the sixteen contemplations, and told her that
she must first hang up the drum at sunset, to solidify her
will for the Western Paradise;[25] when the ancient
worthies [spoke of] not forgetting the Western Paradise
whether sitting or lying down -- surely they knew that
there are buddha-lands everywhere. A person of great
liberation can go where he wishes. But if we are not this
way, we must respectfully follow Buddha's commands
[and seek the Pure Land in the west].

## The Power of Vows

Every morning Lu Wen-cheng paid homage to Buddha
and made this vow: "If they do not believe in the

Buddha, the Dharma, and the Sangha, may my family perish. I hope that generation after generation my sons and grandsons will hold official rank and uphold the Buddha Dharma." The later offspring of the Lu family, like Lu Kung-chu, Lu Hao-wen, and Lu Yung-chung were all famous men of high rank who served Buddha.

Now Lu Wen-cheng just made a vow for good in the human world, and it was answered with what he wished for generation after generation without end. A great world-transcending vow to seek birth in the Pure Land would be even more [efficacious]. The fulfillment of Lu Wen-cheng's vow depended on his descendants, and he could not know whether he would get his wish or not. A vow to seek birth in the Pure Land will be fulfilled with oneself. Thus one will know that if he does not achieve the Pure Land, it is because his own purity and sincerity were not perfect.

In the old days there was a noble family that was supporting a monk. They asked the monk, "After you die, would you be willing to be reborn in our family?" The monk laughed [implying consent], and subsequently was born into that family. In recent times Lord Fan, the border commander, was also [the reincarnation of] a monk his father had supported.

Both stories illustrate how laughing consent given once can lead to incarnation in a powerful family. So how could it be that long accumulated purity and sincerity will not lead to birth in the Pure Land? Cause and effect surely work this way. There's no room for discussion [on this point].

# All Classes Go to the Pure Land

There was once a man who despised the Pure Land [as the easy route to salvation] and did not cultivate it [maintaining that Zen was the way for superior people]. He said, "My type enters office by passing the examinations. How could we purchase official rank?"

Another man answered, "This analogy is wrong. There are nine grades of those who arrive in the Pure Land. Why don't you take the highest: why are you willing to be in the lowest grade? Here we have three hundred people taking the Pure Land 'examination,' and they can be divided into high, middle, and low, and into the nine grades. Why don't you take first prize among them? Why are you willing to be last on the list?

"Being born in the top grade is taking first prize on the Pure Land 'examination.' There is a verse that praises such people:

With faith, vows, and practice fully developed,
Profoundly understanding the principles of the truth,
The Pure Land is wherever they go
As they witness birthlessness.

"In the Zen school such people [are said to have] great penetration and great enlightenment. These are the ones spoken of in the verse [by the Zen adept Layman P'ang]:

'Mind empty, having passed the test, they return home.'"

[Hearing this], the man [who had denigrated the Pure Land] looked defeated and said, "This has melted my doubts."


# One Hundred Thousand Repetitions of "Amitabha" in a Single Day and Night


Tradition has it that the Great Teacher Yen-shou of Yung-ming recited the buddha-name a hundred thousand times in a day and a night.

I once attempted this myself. From the dawn of one day to the dawn of the next, continuing every minute for twenty-four hours, I just barely managed a hundred thousand repetitions. I recited "Amitabha Buddha." If I had been reciting "Hail to Amitabha Buddha," I would not have reached the full number. I did not stop while drinking or eating or dressing or undressing. If there had been the least interruption, I would not have reached the full number. I did not sleep or speak at all: if I had, I would not have reached the full number. [My recitation of the buddha-name] was hurried and pressed, as if chasing someone down a road. There was no time for reciting with careful attention. If I had recited with careful attention, I would not have reached the full number.

Therefore we know that the story of reciting the buddha-name a hundred thousand times in a day and a night was probably meant to suggest the idea of not departing from buddha-name recitation even for an instant; it was not meant to give a set figure of a hundred thousand repetitions.

I am afraid that if those who recite the buddha-name with the mind of faith were to hold to this [number literally as a set standard], it would become a sickness. Thus, to inform you all, I relate the experiment that I undertook.

Some may say that reciting the buddha-name a hundred thousand times in a day and a night is something that the Great Master Yen-shou did in the midst of Zen concentration. If so, this is not something I would know about.

## Why Don't We Read of People Who Were Enlightened Through Reciting the Buddha-Name?

Someone asked, "In the books we see many who attained enlightenment from studying Zen. Why are those who attain enlightenment from reciting the buddha-name so rare that we never hear of them?"

Alas! There are indeed such people, but you have never read of them.

Now those people who study Zen and find the inner truth never make noise and promote themselves. Only after the devas and nagas [dragons] push them forward do they become famous in their own time and thereafter.

Ts'ao-ch'i [Hui-neng, the Sixth Patriarch of Zen] had the mind-seal of [the Fifth Patriarch] Huang-mei, but if he had not commented about the wind and the flag [telling two arguing monks, "It is not the wind that is moving, or the flag that is moving, but your minds that are moving"] he would have [remained unknown] as a netminder for a hunter, and that's all.[26]

Ch'ing-su received the secret prediction [of enlightenment] from Tz'u-ming, but if he had not unexpectedly met him at a lichee tree [and exchanged words that let Tz'u-ming discern his attainments], he would have been an old man at ease in the Zen community, and that's all. How would you have known of him?

The same is true for those who recite the buddha-name with a genuine mind. Their will goes beyond this world as they seek the Pure Land with pure refinement, reciting the buddha-name every moment as if saving themselves when their heads are on fire. Thus they awaken to the Amitabha of inherent nature and comprehend the Pure Land of mind-only. If they hide themselves away their whole lives and do not come forward, you would have no way to know of them.

Anyone who is in the top class born in the Pure Land is a person who has attained enlightenment. [If you want examples of enlightenment through buddha-name recitation], you should read the biographies of those who have gone to the Pure Land.

## One Slip, a Hundred Slips

An ancient said:

If you do not practice in this lifetime, one slip is a hundred slips.

From one slip to a hundred slips: how is it that there are so many slips, that it comes to this many? The sutra says:

It is hard to leave the evil planes of existence [in hell, as a hungry ghost, as an animal], and attain a human body. Having gotten a human body, it is hard to encounter the teaching of enlightenment, the Buddha Dharma.

This being so, it is especially hard to encounter the Dharma-gate of reciting the buddha-name and to believe in it and accept it.

According to what the sutra says, an ant may have gone on being reborn as an ant ever since the time of the Seven Buddhas of antiquity, without escaping from an ant's body. Who knows when it will attain a human body, when it will encounter the Buddha Dharma, and when it will encounter the method of reciting the buddha-name and believe in it and accept it? This is not only a hundred slips, but a thousand slips, ten thousand slips, an endless number of slips. What pain!

## Three Difficulties for Pure Land Belief

Someone posed this question: "Shakyamuni Buddha touched the ground with his toe, and immediately it became a golden world. If Buddha has such powers, why does he not immediately transform this world of ours, the world called Endurance, with its earth and rocks and mountains, with its places filled with filth and with evil, into a land of ultimate bliss, adorned with all manner of precious jewels, and let sentient beings quickly advance to the far reaches of millions and billions of buddha-lands?"

Alas! Buddha cannot deliver beings without the causal conditions for enlightenment. You know this, don't you? Pure causal conditions bring about pure lands. If the minds of sentient beings are not pure, even though the Pure Land exists, how can they get to be born in it?

For example, beings who practice the ten virtues are born as devas, and change hell into heaven. Even though the Tathagata extends his golden arm to pull them up, those sentient beings who practice the ten evils can never ascend to his inner palace.

Therefore, when Buddha drew back his spiritual powers, the momentary golden world turned back into the world of Endurance it had been before.

Someone asked, "In the sutras it is said that one repetition of the buddha-name made with complete sincerity wipes away the sins of eighty trillion eons of birth and death. Does this refer to the level of things and events, or to the level of inner truth?"

The sutra says:

> Invoke the buddha-name once, and [you have] already become buddha [for that moment].

It also says:

> Pay homage to buddha once, and one's feet arrive at the diamond realm, and an atom of dust becomes the seat of a wheel-turning king.

Right now there is no need to talk about things and
events and inner truth. We should just focus on the two
words *complete sincerity*.

Just worry that your mind will not be in a state of
complete sincerity; [if it is], don't worry that sins will
not be wiped away. If it is like this in the event, it will
be like this in inner truth; if it is like this in inner truth,
it will be like this in the event. What is there to doubt?

\*\*\*

Someone else asked, "One person earnestly recites the
buddha-name his whole life, but on the brink of death
regresses for a moment, and consequently does not get to
go to the Pure Land. One person piles up evil his whole
life, but on the brink of death aspires to enlightenment
and recites the buddha-name, and consequently gets to go
to the Pure Land. Why should the good person lose and
the evil person gain?"

Ah! Only one person in a million accumulates evil his
whole life and then achieves correct mindfulness on the
brink of death. Without the roots of goodness from past
lives, on his deathbed he will be harried by pain and
suffering and plunged into darkness and confusion: how
would he be able to generate correct mindfulness? Again,
among good people, only one in a million regresses on the
brink of death. If there is such a person, it must be that
his lifelong buddha-name recitation was done casually and
in vain: it was not pure and earnest. "Pure" means that
his mind was not chaotic and mixed [with other concerns
as he recited the buddha-name]. "Earnest" means that

there were no mental interruptions or breaks [to his recitation].  So [if his recitation was pure and earnest], how could any regression occur?

This being so, those who do evil should come to their senses quickly, and not falsely imagine that they will have this kind of undeserved good fortune on the brink of death.  Those who seek the Pure Land with a genuine mind should be ever more pure and earnest, and not worry that on the brink of death they will regress.

# DIRECT POINTING
# BACK
# TO THE SOURCE

by

Master Tsung-pen

# Preface

The Venerable Shakyamuni Buddha appeared in the world for one great cause: to open up the perception of the buddhas to sentient beings, to enable them to awaken to the Great Path of the real and the eternal.

The people of the world did not comprehend the truth of this, and rejected [Buddha's teaching] as heresy. They were like unfilial children who hate their parents. What a painful thing!

I had lived in seclusion for a long time [trying to find enlightenment], but because my eye for the Path was not clear, for me it was just as the saying goes: "All people feed on it, but few can recognize its flavor." Alas!

A Confucian can pay homage to Buddha and be a true Confucian. Have you not read what Prime Minister Chang Shang-ying said? "Only after I studied Buddhism was I able to understand Confucianism." This is what he meant.

Zen master I-yuan Tsung-pen of Yen-ch'ing studied Confucianism in his youth, and when he grew up followed Buddhism. He had penetrating enlightenment in the school of reality-nature [Zen], and specialized in cultivating Pure Land practice. He was truly one who stood out from the multitude as a man of knowledge, an enlightened teacher. Because he was keen to benefit others, he put together this collection. One day he passed by my abode and invited me to compose a preface for this book.

I urge you people who study the Path, once you have the faith to enter upon it, practice it with all your strength.[27]

You should not stick to the [letter of] the teaching and miss its intent, or take the pointing finger for the moon.

It is all a matter of splitting open an atom of dust and letting a universe of scriptures flow forth from it,[28] to save all living beings and let them achieve correct enlightenment together. How could it depend on one or two texts? Ah! If you really reach this stage, my words too are but sleep talk.

*Preface by Wang Piao, the Layman of the Deer Garden [dated] Buddha's birthday, fourth lunar month of [year missing], Lung Ch'ing era [1567-1572]*

# The Author's Conversion to Pure Land

My parents cared for me. They invited a teacher to come and instruct me, and I began to study the classics [of the Confucian tradition]. My father instructed my teacher to be very strict with me until I mastered the *Book of Poetry* and the *Book of Rites*.

When I was fifteen years old, an older cousin of mine, who was a gentleman living at home without any special talents, died from disease. The body was laid out in an empty hall, and I happened to pass by and see my dead cousin. I was alarmed and assailed with worries and doubts. I exclaimed to myself, "Worldly forms are not solid. Life is like a candle in the wind. When impermanence suddenly arrives, it is impossible to escape."

After this, I wanted to leave home [to become a monk] and study the [Buddhist] Path and transcend the cycle of birth and death. But I did not know where to begin to practice, and in my mind there was still some hesitation.

I came to a tea-house in my neighborhood, and as I was paying homage to a statue of Buddha there, I happened to see a monk sitting upright with an awe-inspiring air about him. I asked him who he was. He said, "I am a wandering Zen man." When I heard him say this, I was overwhelmed with joy, so I immediately invited him to come home with me.

After I had prepared incense and a vegetarian meal and offered him food, I bowed before him and said, "I want to escape from birth and death, but I do not know what method to cultivate."[29]

The Zen man asked me my name and age. I said, "My name is Ch'en Ching-hsiu and I am fifteen years old."

The Zen man praised me saying, "It is rare in the world for one so young to have such a lofty aspiration. Concentrate and listen quietly to what I say, my boy. The only direct road of practice is to recite 'Amitabha Buddha.'"

I said, "How can one transcend birth and death by reciting 'Amitabha Buddha'?"

The Zen man said, "Believe what Buddha said. The best method for escaping suffering is to recite the buddha-name. If you do not recite the buddha-name, it will be difficult to escape birth and death."

I asked, "Where does the method of reciting the buddha-name come from?"

The Zen man answered, "The method of reciting the buddha-name is recorded in more than one sutra. Among the countless scriptures, there is not one that does not contain the method of reciting the buddha-name. If you practice according to this method, you are sure to be born in the Pure Land."

I asked, "How much merit is there in reciting the buddha-name, that one may thereby be born in the Pure Land?"

The Zen man replied, "If you offered to the buddhas and bodhisattvas and pratyekas and shravakas all the jewels in the world, the merit of this would be very great, but it would not equal the merit of urging people to recite the buddha-name even once."

I asked, "How could one repetition of the buddha-name be better?"

The Zen man answered, "The *Treatise on Birth in the Buddha-Land* says:

> If a man could walk a thousand miles a day from birth, and lived a thousand years, and all the lands he traversed were filled with jewels, and he offered these jewels to Buddha, it would not equal the merit of a person in the later evil ages who could invoke even once the name of Amitabha Buddha.

"If invoking the buddha-name oneself is this meritorious, how much the more so, to encourage others to recite the buddha-name!"

I asked, "Even though the virtues of Buddha are like this, how could ordinary people, with so much bad karma, be able to attain birth in the Pure Land in one lifetime by reciting the buddha-name?"

The Zen man answered, "The *Sixteen Contemplations of Amitabha Sutra (Meditation Sutra)* says:

> One perfectly sincere repetition of 'Hail to Amitabha Buddha' wipes out the grievous sins of eight billion eons of birth and death.[30]

"Even someone who has committed serious sins throughout his life can get to be born in the Pure Land, if as he is about to die he recites 'Amitabha Buddha' ten times. How much the more so for someone who has kept a vegetarian diet and maintained the precepts and recited the buddha-name his whole life long."[31]

I asked, "Why does Amitabha Buddha have such vast merit and such far-reaching vows?"

The Zen man replied, "The *Greater Amitabha Sutra* says:

One day the expression on the face of Shakyamuni Buddha changed. His constant attendant Ananda thought this was strange and asked him about it. Buddha said, 'Excellent! Your question is better than giving offerings to all the shravakas and pratyekas in the world, and making gifts to all the devas and humans and other living creatures down to the humblest insects. Even if you did this for many eons, it would not equal a billionth part of the merit of your question. Why so? Because due to your question, all creatures from the king of the devas, to the human beings, to the humblest insects will gain liberation.'

"This was the time when Shakyamuni Buddha was first about to speak of Amitabha Buddha. This was on his mind, and so it showed on his face, which was different from normal. Thus we see that Amitabha Buddha's influence on Shakyamuni Buddha was certainly extraordinary. How much the more so is his influence on sentient beings!

"Observe.   When Amitabha Buddha first made his
vows he said, 'When I become a buddha, my name will
sound through the ten directions. Humans and devas will
rejoice to hear it, and all come to be born in my land.
Even those in hell and hungry ghosts and animals will be
born in my land.' Thus we know that Amitabha saves all
in the six planes of existence in the Triple World.

"Right now Amitabha Buddha is in the Land of
Ultimate Bliss in the west, and he is also in all the worlds
of the ten directions teaching and transforming countless
numbers of devas and humans, and all creatures down to
the humblest insects ... If Buddha is saving even the lowly
insects like this, how much the more so is he saving
human beings!  Amitabha also vowed:

> Those who invoke my name are sure to be born in the
> Pure Land.  If it is not so, I swear not to become a
> buddha.

"Thus, Amitabha delivers sentient beings without end.
If people wholeheartedly take refuge with Amitabha, they
will be born in his land.  From this we can infer that the
merit of reciting the buddha-name is truly inconceivable.
Amitabha Buddha also said:

> If there are sentient beings who want to be born in my
> land, those of the highest class must use the mind of
> compassion and not kill living beings;  they must
> cherish and protect all creatures with awareness;  they
> must practice all the precepts;  they must read and
> recite the Great Vehicle scriptures and understand their
> highest meaning;  they must have deep understanding

of true principles and support the Buddha, Dharma and Sangha; they must be filial to their parents and respect them; they must be merciful to the poor and suffering; they must teach and transform sentient beings and add to their power with the food of the Dharma; they must make offerings to the spirits; they must refrain from all forms of evil and faithfully practice all forms of virtue.

If they recite the buddha-name while acting like this, they are sure to be born in the highest class in the Pure Land, and eventually become buddhas. If their strength is not sufficient for this, then for the time being they should firmly uphold a vegetarian diet and maintain the precepts, and singlemindedly recite the buddha-name. If they can recite the buddha-name from moment to moment without a break, they will be born in the Pure Land, and not in the lowest class there.

"This Dharma-Gate [of buddha-name recitation] does not discriminate between wise and ignorant, or high ranking and lowly, or rich and poor. It does not distinguish between male and female or old and young or monks and nuns and laypeople. It does not matter if you have practiced it for a long time or have just recently started. Everyone can recite the buddha-name.

"The guidelines for reciting the buddha-name are not rigid. You can recite the buddha-name in a loud voice or a low voice, while doing ablutions or while making prostrations. You can recite the buddha-name while gathering in the mind, while meditating, while contemplating the concept of buddha, while counting beads. You can recite the buddha-name while walking or standing or sitting quietly or lying on your side. You can recite the buddha-name silently or aloud. You can recite the buddha-name a thousand times or ten thousand times. It is all the same mindfulness of buddha. The only thing that is essential is to have definite faith, and to seek birth in the Pure Land.

"If you can actually practice the recitation like this, then there is no need to seek elsewhere for an enlightened teacher.[32] As the saying goes, 'Steering the boat is entirely up to the person who holds the tiller.' Those who arrive mount to the Land of Peaceful Nurturing [Amitabha's Pure Land] together."

\*\*\*

I asked, "People in the world often say that they are tied down by family affairs and wrapped up in worldly tasks, and that they will wait until they are old to recite the buddha-name. Please comment on this kind of talk."

The Zen man said, "How painful! What foolish, lying words! Haven't you read what Zen master Ssu-hsin said?

Some people in the world have mountains of wealth and precious jewels. Wives and concubines fill their homes to delight them day and night. How could they not want to live forever in the world? But what can they do about it? The road ahead is limited, the darkness presses in upon them. When the command comes they go: no delay is allowed. Old Yama [the King of Death] does not obey human sentiments. The Demon King of Impermanence has no face.

As everyone has seen and heard with their own eyes and ears: how many have died in the neighboring streets and lanes, how many relatives and household members and friends and brothers, how many in the prime of life, how many young people? Haven't you heard the ancient's saying? "Do not wait until you are old before you study the Path. The isolated graves are all the tombs of young people.

"Ssu-hsin also said:

From their early years, men search for wives and rear children and manage their businesses and endure all sorts of troubles and pains. Suddenly the vital energy in their heart is cut off. Unavoidably one day everything stops. If there are filial sons and grandsons, they give a vegetarian feast for a few monks to read the scriptures, they burn paper money and make the proper funeral offerings, and weep and wail. They are remembering papa and mama.

If the children are no good, as soon as the parents die, before the bones are even cold, they are already digging out the wealth and selling off the fields and gardens to indulge their whims and enjoy themselves. If we look at it like this, what was the great urgency [to accumulate possessions]? Your descendants will have their own good fortune: don't worry about them.

"Ssu-hsin also quoted an ancient worthy who said:

A cold laugh for the rich family's patriarch. He is busy as can be managing his enterprises. In his storehouses, weevils are in the grain; in his treasuries, the cords on which the coins are strung are rotting away. All day long he holds the scales [weighing his rent receipts]; at night by lamp light he figures his accounts. His body is like a puppet. Don't let the strings break, old man!

"Such pains Ssu-hsin took to warn people! Would he let you occupy yourself with worldly affairs and wait until you are old before you start to recite the buddha-name?"

*\*\*\**

"You should consider this: how long can a person's life in the world last? In the blink of an eye, it passes. Take advantage of the time before you are old. While you are free from illness, mobilize your body and mind, and put aside worldly affairs. If you have one day's time, recite the buddha-name for a day. If you have an hour's free time, cultivate the Pure Land for an hour. When we are on the brink of death, whether we die well or die badly depends on how we have prepared in advance. [If we have been reciting the buddha-name], the road ahead is secure. If not, then it is too late for regrets. Think about it!

"Happily, it is very easy to recite 'Amitabha Buddha' and be born in the Pure Land. Although people in the world cannot avoid taking care of family affairs, they should [set aside some time] in the morning and evening to burn incense and recite the buddha-name.

"This method of buddha-name recitation can be practiced by everyone. It is like lighting a candle in a room that has been dark for a thousand years: once the candle shines, the room is lit. Thus, even a butcher can put down his killing knife and practice it.

"The means by which [buddha-name recitation] is practiced is not hard, and it does not interfere with ordinary affairs. For those in office, it does not interfere with official business. For scholars, it does not interfere with studying books. For merchants, it does not interfere with buying and selling. For farmers, it does not interfere with plowing and planting. For wives, it does not interfere with women's work. For government clerks, it does not interfere with legal duties. For monks, it does not interfere with studying Zen. It does not interfere with any activity.

"You can recite the buddha-name and pay homage to buddha in the morning or in the evening. When you are busy, steal a little free time [to recite the buddha-name]. Recite the buddha-name every day a thousand times or a hundred times or three hundred times or five hundred times or only ten times.

"All that is important is that you dedicate [the merit gained to the Pure Land] and make vows to go to the Western Paradise. If you can genuinely do this, then you are sure to be born in the Pure Land.

"Chen, my boy, if you keep a vegetarian diet and uphold discipline and recite the buddha-name with pure energy and a unified mind, and if you are not [then] born in the Pure Land, then I will surely [gladly] fall into the hell where tongues are plucked out."

Seeing the Zen man take such a grave oath, I was very impressed, and fell on my knees to give homage to him for instructing me in the method of reciting the buddha-name.

The Zen man said, "Even in a hundred million eons, I could not say all there is to say about the Pure Land teaching. Therefore I have briefly described it in a few words. An ancient worthy said, 'Superior people decide once, and understand everything. With the average and below average sort, the more they hear, the more they don't believe.' How true these words are!

"As for people who practice with true faith being born in the Pure Land in the west, this is not something that you just say you will do, then quit -- you must take it as a great mission. If you fully believe, then from this day forward, you will generate great bravery and great energy.

"Don't ask whether you understand or not, whether you see reality-nature or not.[33] Just hold to the phrase 'Hail to Amitabha Buddha' as if you are up on the Polar Mountain and cannot be shaken.

"This mindfulness of buddha is your fundamental teacher. This mindfulness of buddha is the precious sword which cuts down all heresies. This mindfulness of buddha is the bright lamp that dispels the darkness. This mindfulness of buddha is the great ship for crossing the ocean of suffering. This mindfulness of buddha is the best way to escape birth and death. This mindfulness of buddha is the direct route out of the Triple World. This mindfulness of buddha is the Amitabha of inherent nature and the Pure Land of mind-only.

"You must keep your attention on this phrase 'Amitabha Buddha' and not let it slip away. Let it appear

before you from moment to moment and never leave
your mind.

"Recite the buddha-name like this when you have
nothing to do, and recite the buddha-name like this when
you are busy. Recite the buddha-name like this when you
are happy and at ease, and when you are sick and in pain.
Recite the buddha-name like this when you are living, and
recite the buddha-name like this as you are dying.

"If your mindfulness of buddha is clear, then there is
no need to ask anyone else the way home. As the saying
goes, 'If there is no other thought but Amitabha, then
without even snapping your fingers, you arrive in the
Western Paradise.'"

The Zen man instructed me further, telling me, "Now
I will give you the teaching on the ten realms. You
should instruct those who come after you with this
teaching, so that they can make energetic progress,
cultivate practice, and together achieve the fruits of
buddhahood."

I replied, "I will disseminate this teaching widely to
later generations, in hopes of being of some assistance to
the future."

The Zen man said, "Very good! Very good! "The ten
realms are the realm of the buddhas (the enlightened
ones), the realm of the bodhisattvas (the enlightening
beings), the realm of the pratyeka buddhas (the solitary
illuminates), the realm of the shravakas (the literalist
disciples), the realm of the devas (the heavens), the realm
of the human beings, the realm of the asuras (the
demigods), the realm of the hungry ghosts, the realm of
the animals, and the realm of the hells. The ten realms are

all present in the One Mind, and experienced according to the karma one creates.

"According to the causal basis you create, the results you have created are returned to you. Thus, practicing good and practicing evil are worldly causes, and the six planes of existence in the Triple World are worldly results. Maintaining discipline and reciting the buddha-name are world-transcending causes, and the Pure Land and becoming buddha are world-transcending results.

"In the paths of humans and devas, making merit is foremost. In the sea of birth and death, reciting the buddha-name is number one. Those who want to enjoy the happiness of devas and humans without cultivating merit, those who want to escape birth and death without reciting the buddha-name, are like birds who want to fly without wings, like trees that want to flourish without roots. It cannot be done.

"You must take reciting the buddha-name as the correct basis, and making merit as an auxiliary factor. Cultivating both merit and wisdom, you will achieve correct enlightenment.

"Thus, causes encompass the sea of results, and results extend back through the causal source.[34] There is no gap between cause and effect: from beginning to end, they are never obscured. Why? If the form is straight, the shadow is upright. If the sound is harmonious, the echo is pleasant. You must realize that if the cause is genuine, the result will not be false. What you do right now is the cause; what you experience at death is the result. If you do evil, then evil realms will appear. If you recite the buddha-name, then the realm of buddha will arrive spontaneously.

"Haven't you read what it says in the *Flower Ornament (Avatamsaka) Sutra?*

If you want to fully know all the buddhas of past, present and future, you must contemplate the nature of the realm of reality. Everything is created by Mind alone."

I asked, "What method do we cultivate in order to reach the realm of the buddhas?"

The Zen man said, "You must realize that all sentient beings in the six planes of existence have buddha-nature. True thusness is everywhere equal. View all sentient beings as sharing a single essence. Think of them like buddhas, like your parents. Do not separate enemies and kinsmen -- save them all. For all time to come, carry out the work of universal salvation practiced by the Bodhisattva Samantabhadra. If you can practice according to this method, then you will be equal to the buddhas."

I asked, "What method do we cultivate in order to reach the realm of the bodhisattvas?"

The Zen man answered, "By giving, you transcend stinginess and craving. By upholding discipline, you transcend destructiveness and sin. By patient forbearance, you transcend anger. By energetic progress, you transcend laziness and sloth. By meditative concentration, you transcend oblivion and scattering. By wisdom, you transcend ignorance. If you can practice according to this method, then you will be equal to the bodhisattvas."

I asked, "What method do we cultivate in order to reach only the realm of the pratyeka buddhas, the solitary enlightened ones?"

The Zen man answered, "People of the middle vehicle enjoy solitude and think stillness is best. Though they know the causal conditions for all phenomena, they do not practice universal salvation, so they only reach the realm of the pratyekas."

I asked, "What method do we cultivate in order to reach only the realm of the shravakas, the literalist disciples?"

The Zen man answered, "People of the lesser vehicle fear birth and death like a ferocious beast. They escape it alone, without concern for those who come after them. They wish to escape the Triple World quickly, and seek nirvana for themselves. Because of this, they only reach the realm of the shravakas."

I asked, "What method do we cultivate in order to be born in the plane of the devas, the celestial beings?"

The Zen man answered, "By cultivating the ten virtues, one attains birth in the realm of the devas."

\*\*\*

I asked, "What method do we cultivate in order to again attain the human level?"

The Zen man answered, "By firmly upholding the five precepts [against murder, theft, lying, sexual excess, and intoxication], one will attain birth in the human realm."

I asked, "What bad karma do we create to cause us to descend into the realm of the asuras, the jealous demigods?"

The Zen man answered, "If a person cultivates good karma, but constantly harbors the attitude of competitiveness and anger and arrogance, he falls into the realm of the asuras."

I asked, "What bad karma do we create to cause us to descend into the realm of the hungry ghosts?"

The Zen man answered, "Selfish craving, feeding oneself by deceiving the group, leads to falling into the realm of the hungry ghosts."

I asked, "What bad karma do we create that causes us to fall into the animal realm?"

The Zen man answered, "If one creates the karma of ignorance, stupidity, error and evil, one will surely fall into the animal realm."

I asked, "What bad karma do we create that causes us to fall into hell?"

The Zen man answered, "If one disrupts or slanders the Buddha, Dharma, and Sangha, and commits a multitude of evils, one will definitely fall into hell.

"In sum, these ten realms depend on what people do and what they practice."

***

I bowed down to give thanks to the Zen man and said, "If not for good fortune in past lives, how could I have encountered an enlightened teacher to instruct me?"

The Zen man bade me farewell and said, "If you have any doubts that are not yet resolved, you should read [Pure Land books like] *The Precious Mirror of the Lotus School, Pointing out the Way Back to the Pure Land,* Lung-

shu's *Pure Land Texts, Where the Myriad Virtues Return,*
Chih-i's *Treatise on Ten Doubts about the Pure Land,* T'ien-
ju's *Questions about the Pure Land,*[35] Shen-ch'i's *Verses on
the Land of Peaceful Nurturing,* and the *Treatise to Resolve
Doubts about the Pure Land.* You can also read any of the
sutras that extol the Pure Land."

I said, "I respectfully accept your instructions, and will
faithfully carry them out."

[The text continues:] The story of Tsung-pen's leaving
home and studying is long and is not recorded.

# A Mirror for Studying Zen

There is nothing else particularly special about the
method of studying the Path: simply cleanse the sense
faculties and sense objects, and make enlightenment the
standard.

Good people, if you want to cultivate supreme
enlightenment, you must firmly uphold discipline and
maintain a vegetarian diet. If you do not strictly uphold
discipline, you will never achieve enlightenment. What is
the reason? Discipline is the foremost of the myriad
practices, the foundation of the six perfections. It is like
building a house: first you make a solid foundation.
Without a solid foundation, you build in vain.

As for discipline, this means the three combined
disciplines of the Great Vehicle. One is the discipline
covering codes of conduct, that cuts off all evils. That is,
"Do not commit any of the forms of evil." One is the
discipline covering good practices, that gathers together all

forms of good. That is, "Faithfully practice the many virtues." One is the discipline of benefiting all sentient beings, so all beings are saved. That is, "Universally deliver sentient beings."[36]

These three combined disciplines are the disciplines by which bodhisattvas become buddhas. Only if a person possesses these three disciplines can he cultivate Zen. Without the mentality [of these three combined disciplines], it does no good to study Zen.

Haven't you read what it says in the *Brahma Net Sutra*?

If sentient beings accept the discipline of the buddhas, they will enter into the station of the buddhas.

Could it be otherwise?

The buddhas and patriarchs say, "Discipline can engender meditative concentration, and meditative concentration can engender wisdom. With wisdom, you illuminate mind. Illuminating mind, you see reality-nature, and become buddha. Being an enlightened teacher or a buddha always depends on this discipline."

The business of studying Zen is the epitome of the mystic device of transcendence. It is not possible for those who take it easy.[37]

You must generate great bravery and great energy. You also must stop thoughts, forget entangling objects, and gather in your seeing and hearing and turn them back [onto inherent reality]. You must take your everyday views of good and evil, your likes and dislikes, and your sentiments of affirmation and denial, and totally sweep them away.

[Zen study] is like a sharp sword cutting through a skein of thread: when one thread is cut, all are cut. It is like cutting the mooring rope and casting off in a boat, and sailing away. It is like one man battling ten thousand men: there is no time to blink, no time to hesitate in doubt.

If you can really generate this kind of adamant, fierce willpower, you will have the mettle to study Zen.

Once you have the mettle to study Zen, take hold of the phrase "Amitabha Buddha" as if you are resting on the Polar Mountain and cannot be shaken. Concentrate your mind and unify your attention. Recite the buddha-name a few times, turn the light back and observe yourself, asking: Who is this one reciting the buddha-name?

As you come to grips with it, you must see where this mindfulness of buddha, this recitation of the buddha-name, is arising from. After a long time, you will see through this mindfulness. Add doubt on top of doubt: ask yourself who, ultimately, is this one asking "who is the one reciting the buddha-name?"

When you get here, hold the rope tight and don't let go. It is like seeing a mortal enemy. Hold tight: you must comprehend correctly. There is no room for hesitating in thought, no time for discussions. If you study Zen like this, eventually you will succeed.

If you are as yet unable to act like this, listen further to some more talk. The method of work in studying Zen [can be described with the following metaphors].

It is like a person at the bottom of a well a thousand feet deep. Morning and night he thinks of only one thing: he wants to find a way out of the well. He has no other thought.

It is like when you have lost something that is of crucial importance: you look for it everywhere from morning till evening. If you cannot find it, you think of it carefully, sighing with concern.

It is like a cat hunting a rat, unified within and without [in rapt concentration].

It is like crossing a bridge made out of a single plank — you are extremely careful.

If you use your mind like this, then oblivion and scattering naturally recede. Whether you are walking, standing, sitting, or lying down, [do your meditation work] as if you are holding an infant: you cannot make any sudden violent moves.

Therefore, to pluck the pearl [from the bottom of the water], you must still the waves. To get the pearl when the water is moving is sure to be hard. When you have stilled the water and it is clear, the mind-pearl appears by itself ... Thus the *Complete Enlightenment Sutra* says:

> Unobstructed pure wisdom is always born on the basis of samadhi, of stable meditative concentration.

If you can really carry out your meditation work like this, then you will have meditative concentration in hand.

Even when samadhi appears before you, you must not abide in "dead-tree" samadhi.[38] You must study the Great Matter [of enlightenment] until you illuminate it completely, and achieve perfect omniscience. An ancient worthy said, "Don't just forget your physical body and deaden your mind. This is the most serious of hard-to-cure ailments." To succeed, you must plumb the depths of the source. Then you will see reality-nature and recognize the natural reality. Of this it has been said: "Take a step forward from the top of the hundred foot high pole. Hanging from the cliff, let go. After annihilation, you return to life — only then can you be called a person who completely understands things."

If good scenes appear before you [as you meditate], you should not be happy, or the delusion of happiness may enter your mind. If bad scenes appear before you, you should not be vexed, or the delusion of vexation may enter your mind. You must realize that such scenes do not come from outside: all are born from being sunk in oblivion, or are brought about by karmic consciousness. All that the eyes see and the ears hear is false — don't get attached to it! Keep on making energetic progress ...[39]

If intellectual understanding appears before you, do not accept it. Quickly sweep it away.[40] If you abide in the realm of intellectual knowledge, you are burying your original face. An ancient worthy said:

The Buddha Dharma is not fresh fish — don't worry that it will rot away. It is like peeling an onion. You peel off one layer, and there is another layer. You peel off that layer, and there is yet another layer. Keep on peeling until there is no place left to begin, and then you will achieve unity.

After this, [whatever you do], putting on clothes, eating food, going to the toilet, moving or keeping still, talking or keeping silent, none of it is not the one Amitabha Buddha. From this mind there radiates a light which shines through the ten directions like the sun at high noon lighting up the sky, like a clear mirror on its stand. Before another moment goes by, suddenly you achieve true enlightenment. Not only do you understand this one great matter, you penetrate from top to bottom all the stories of the buddhas and enlightened teachers and understand completely all the teachings of enlightenment and all the phenomena of the world.

When you reach this stage, you still cannot abide in it or get attached to it. You must seek an adept to certify your enlightenment, find accord with him, and get his seal of approval.

After you get the seal of approval, you do not posit holy or ordinary, you forget both grasping and rejecting, you do not speak of heaven and hell or differentiate between south, north, east, and west. The whole universe is your own Amitabha. All of space is the Pure Land of mind-only.

Then you will be able to manifest the land of the Jewel King on the tip of a hair and turn the wheel of the Great Dharma while seated in an atom of dust. You will receive and guide future people and support those in the last age. Only a Zen person like this is a great person beyond convention, a hero who goes beyond the crowd.

If you are not yet like this, then for now rely on the power of the vows of Amitabha Buddha, and seek birth in the Pure Land. Why? I am afraid that at the end of your life, delusory objects will appear before you and your limbs will be in confusion. Then you will be unable to ward off [delusion], and you will inevitably go off again following your karmic entanglements. You must genuinely recite the buddha-name and cultivate both merit and wisdom and place your thoughts on the Pure Land ...

# Zen is Hard,
# Pure Land is Easy

*Question*
In the world there are people who hold exclusively to Zen meditation cases -- koans -- and make people do their meditation work on them. They hope to awaken to the Path through studying Zen, and do not vow to be born in the Pure Land. What about this teaching?

*Answer*
People of sharp faculties and superior wisdom are capable of real Zen study and genuine awakening. But if there is the slightest error, [exclusive reliance on Zen] becomes a big mistake.

*Question*
How do we know this is a mistake?

*Answer*
The mistake comes in not awakening and going on as before revolving in the cycle of birth and death. It is better to cultivate practice by reciting the buddha-name and be sure of finding a direct road to birth in the Pure Land.

It is not that enlightened teachers do not teach you to study Zen -- it's that they are afraid you will not recite the buddha-name. What is the reason? Awakening to the Path by studying Zen is hard. Being born in the Pure Land by reciting the buddha-name is easy.

Haven't you heard the saying of the ancient worthy?

To study Zen it is necessary to completely comprehend birth and death, and not two or three in a hundred succeed. If they seek birth in the Pure Land by reciting the buddha-name, not one in ten thousand fails.

As the saying goes:

With Zen but without Pure Land, nine out of ten go wrong.

Is it not so?

Moreover, studying Zen does not obstruct reciting the buddha-name, and reciting the buddha-name does not obstruct studying Zen.

Now the relative difficulty and ease of Zen and Pure Land is clear. There are indeed eighty-four thousand methods including the direct pointing [of Zen], but none of them is as good as the one phrase "Amitabha Buddha." Although there are seventeen hundred Zen koans, they do not equal the one phrase "Amitabha Buddha."

In the teaching of Amitabha Buddha, there is both sudden and gradual, both inner truth and apparent manifestation. People of superior faculties and wisdom take it up directly, see reality-nature and become buddhas. The middle and lower sort are incapable of sudden transcendence: they rely on the power of Amitabha Buddha and attain birth in the Pure Land. For this reason, the teaching of reciting the buddha-name is superior to all other teachings. The other meditation cases are not one percent as effective as the buddha-remembrance meditation case ["Who is the one reciting the buddha-name?"] What is the reason? If they were equally as effective, then all the past, present, and future buddhas of the ten directions would not have extolled Amitabha Buddha, and all the countless scriptures would not point the way to the Pure Land in the west ...

In olden times, the Tathagata [Shakyamuni] said to Maudgalyayana:

> It is like the floating plants in the myriad ever-flowing rivers. The ones ahead do not look at the ones behind them, and the ones behind do not look at the ones ahead of them, but all of them meet in the ocean. Worldly life is also like this. Though some people are powerful and high-ranking and rich and happy and independent, not one of them manages to avoid old age and sickness and death. Because they do not believe in the Buddha's scriptures, they are unable to be born in the thousand buddha-lands. Therefore I say that the land of Amitabha is easy to go to and easy to attain. But people do not cultivate the practice needed to be born there. Instead they serve the ninety-six kinds of heretical paths. I call them people without eyes or ears.

In the records of birth in the Pure Land and the biographies of eminent monks, [we read that] both worthy people and ignorant people are born in the Pure Land, and both people of ancient times and people of today go there. All of them totally abandoned impure lands and all of them went to the Pure Land. They were reborn [in a lotus flower] in the Seven Jewel Pond [in the Pure Land] and left behind the pains of incarnation in a womb. They transcended ordinary existence and entered into the sagely realm. They attained the Path and witnessed Reality. Without going through three incalculable eons, they achieved the Path of the Buddha. Isn't the power of [Amitabha] Buddha inconceivable?

If you want to rise above the cycle of birth and death forever, and attain the bliss of nirvana, you need the Dharma-Gate of birth in the Pure Land. Why?

This world of ours called "Endurance" is a defiled realm, where all forms of suffering are assembled: if you seek the Path here, it is hard to succeed.

The Pure Land is a realm of bliss, where all good things are gathered together, from which there is no falling back.[41] If you invoke the buddha-name, all the buddhas will protect you and you will be born in the Pure Land. As for generating enlightenment, [in the Pure Land] the light of Amitabha shines on you and promotes your progress, the bodhisattvas and arhats accompany you, and the water birds and forest trees are all reciting the buddha-name. You constantly hear the wondrous Dharma in your ears. In your mind, craving and anger are suddenly cut off, and there is happiness without end. Your lifespan is not limited to one [earthly] lifetime ...

Alas! The faith of those with the first aspiration for enlightenment (bodhi mind) is shallow: without the power of Buddha, it is hard for them to advance in their practice. The vows of our [Amitabha] Buddha are profound: all who have an affinity with him are gathered in.

Good people, since ancient times the buddhas and enlightened teachers have established teachings and shown the method of reciting the buddha-name. Why then do [certain] followers of Zen today not believe in birth in the Pure Land? Cultivating Pure Land practice does not interfere with studying Zen, so why should those who study Zen denigrate it and not cultivate it?

## True Vows

Pure Land master Tz'u-chao said:

Practice without vows means the practice will be isolated. Vows without practice means the vows will be empty. If you have neither practice nor vows, you live in the world in vain. If you have both practice and vows, you enter directly into uncontrived reality.

Thus vows are the basis of the buddhas' and patriarchs' cultivation of Pure Land practice. Why? Understanding is guided by wisdom, practice flourishes because of vows. When vows and practice are given equal weight, understanding and wisdom are both present.

To vow [to do something] means to want to do it. If you want to be born in the Pure Land in the west, if you want to see Amitabha Buddha, you must make a vow: only then can you go to the Pure Land. Without the intent of the vow, the roots of goodness will disappear. The *Flower Ornament (Avatamsaka) Sutra* says:

Those who do not make great vows are controlled by delusion. All forms of service to Buddha arise from vows. If you want to attain the Supreme Path, you must attain the perfection of vows.

This is why Samantabhadra's vows are vast and boundless as the ocean, and Amitabha took forty-eight vows.

Thus we know that all the buddhas of the ten directions and all the sages from ancient times onward have all achieved enlightenment on the basis of the power of their vows. The *Perfection of Wisdom Treatise* says:

> People cultivate a little bit of merit and a little bit of discipline, but they do not know the correct basis for liberation. They have heard talk of the pleasures of humans and devas, and in their minds they are always vowing to enjoy them after the end of their [present] lives and be reborn as humans or devas. This will be brought about by the power of their vows. Bodhisattvas seek birth in the Pure Land. This is a matter of having a firm will and strong vows -- only then will they attain it.

The *Perfection of Wisdom Treatise* also says:

> Even though people have only cultivated a little bit of merit, because they have the power of their vows, they will attain great rewards.

The *Great Adornment Treatise* says:

> [Being born in] a buddha-land is a great affair. It cannot be achieved through the merit of isolated practice. It requires the power of vows as an aid: only

then can you attain birth in a buddha-land and see Buddha.

The *Flower Ornament (Avatamsaka) Sutra* chapter on practice and vows [of Samantabhadra] says:

> When a person is on the brink of death, in his last moment, all his faculties disintegrate, and he is bereft of all his kinfolk; all his powers are lost and none of his possessions remain with him. The only thing he does not relinquish is the power of his vows: at all times, they lead him forward. In an instant, he attains birth in the Land of Ultimate Bliss.

From this we can infer that we must make vows all the time to honor birth in the Pure Land, and pray every day that we will not regress. Thus it is said, "The Gate to the Dharma is vast and great, but without vows we cannot go through it." This being so, Buddha fulfills people's vows according to [the condition of] their minds.

Alas! These days we often see people who aspire to join a Buddhist congregation because of the pain of illness, or to repay their parents, or to protect their families and homes, or who maintain a vegetarian diet because they fear [the consequences of] their wrongdoings. Though they have faith, they do not have practice or vows. Though they say they are reciting the buddha-name, they have not comprehended the basic root [of buddha-remembrance, namely, vows].

All those who cultivate good causes do so in order to repay promises they have made. Those who take vows to recite the buddha-name and seek birth in the Pure Land rarely do so for the sake of their own [liberation from] birth and death.  Usually when they burn incense and candles at shrines, or make dedications and transfer merit, it is only to announce their offerings to the spirits, to ward off disaster or extend their lives.  They go against the fundamental idea of repentance explained in the scriptures and do not accord with the basic vow of the buddhas.  Even if they chant the scriptures throughout their lives, they do not understand their meaning, and they misuse their effort.  This is what is called "counting the treasures of others all day long but not having half a cent for oneself."  The reason why such people do not go to the Pure Land when they die is that they have no [real] practice or vows.

There is another sort of ignorant people who when they take refuge with Buddha and receive the precepts, burn incense in front of the Three Jewels and swear that if they break the precepts they will willingly accept [all sorts of dire punishments], fall into the clutches of the government in this lifetime, and after they die descend into the three mires [to be reborn as hungry ghosts, as animals, or in hell].  Alas!  These people do not know that the buddhas and enlightened teachers operated with compassion, and never taught people to act like this.  This is all the fault of misguided teachers, who wrongly consider taking oaths on pain of punishment to be making vows.  What utter confusion!

I think of these people with pity, and urge them to take correct vows along with us, vowing to seek birth in the Pure Land, and to become buddhas together.  They say, "We are ordinary people.  How can we dare to hope

to be born in the Pure Land and become buddhas? If we
thought this, it would be false imagination."

I answer them: Not so. "Buddha" means "enlightened
one." The Pure Land is Mind. Who does not possess this
Mind? If you awaken, you are a buddha; if you are
deluded, you are an ordinary being.

Worldly people turn their backs on enlightenment and
join with the dusts of sensory experience, to revolve in
the Triple World through various forms of birth in the
six planes of existence. Their good and bad karmic
connections, and the good and bad results they receive,
are all because they falsely accept the physical body as
their true body and the sensory world as really existing.
They flow along day and night following these illusory
objects. Never for a moment do they realize that they
should turn the light around, keep a vegetarian diet and
maintain discipline, and recite the buddha-name.

From birth to old age, all they do is worry that their
family affairs will not be taken care of and that their
wealth will not be enough to please them. The more
they have, the more they seek; the more they covet, the
more dissatisfied they are.

Though they claim they are accumulating virtue and
serving Buddha and paying homage to Buddha and
making merit and offering incense, all that they are
hoping for [by doing this] is [to gain] riches and high rank
and glory and eternal life. As soon as they do a little bit
of good, they are hoping that it will guarantee them full
granaries and prolific silkworms and famous descendants
and fertile livestock. As soon as something goes against
their wishes, they resent Buddha for not safeguarding

them. Day after day they happily add to their wealth,
saying that this is the response they have earned from the
devas and nagas.

Such covetous calculations are indeed false thinking.
Though these people claim that they recite the buddha-name
and seek birth in the Pure Land, since they are entertaining
these false thoughts, are they not very deluded?

Some say that making merit all belongs in the
category of contrived action, and is a worldly, defiled
causal basis, not a practice of the uncontrived
world-transcending Path. You children of Buddha should
think this over carefully. Today you have a causal
connection and have gotten to meet with the Buddha
Dharma. You must investigate the root: don't argue over
the branches.

Turn the light around for a moment and cultivate the
world-transcending Dharma.

Vow to abandon this world "Endurance" and vow to
be born in the Pure Land, as if you were a long time
traveller in another land who longs to return home.

How can this vow to be born in the Pure Land and
become a buddha be compared to the false thinking of
ordinary people? Haven't you read what it says in *Pure
Land Repentance?*

> I vow that when I am about to die, I will clear away all
> obstruction, and see Amitabha Buddha face to face, and
> be born in the land of peace and bliss.

As the saying goes, "one morning you step onto the
road to the future, and for the first time you
realize that you have been misusing mind."

# Pure Land and the Bodhisattva Path
## according to
## the Great Teacher Chih-i of T'ien-t'ai

*Question*

The work of the buddhas and bodhisattvas is great compassion. In order to rescue sentient beings, they must vow to be born in the Triple World, in the world of the five corruptions, in the midst of the three mires, to save the suffering beings there. How could they seek birth in the Pure Land, to put themselves at peace while abandoning sentient beings. How could they be without compassion, and concentrate only on benefitting themselves? This would block the bodhisattva path.

*Answer*

There are two kinds of bodhisattvas. One kind have cultivated the bodhisattva path for a long time and attained the [perfect] forbearance [that comes with realizing that all] phenomena are unborn. This objection would apply to them.

The second kind have not yet attained [perfect forbearance]; this includes ordinary people with the first aspiration for enlightenment. These "ordinary people bodhisattvas" must never be apart from the perfection of the Buddha's power of forbearance: only then can they dwell in the Triple World, in the world of evil, and save suffering beings. Thus the *Perfection of Wisdom Treatise* says:

> It is impossible for ordinary people in bondage to have the mind of great compassion and vow to be born in evil worlds to save sentient beings.

Why so? In evil worlds, the afflictions are powerful. Since ordinary people themselves lack the power of forbearance, their minds would follow objects and they would be tied down by sound and form. Since they themselves would fall into the three mires, how could they save other sentient beings?

Even if they [avoided the rebirth as animals, hungry ghosts, or hell-beings, and] were born as humans, the path of the sages would be hard for them to find. Perhaps by upholding discipline and cultivating merit they would be born as human and get to be kings or great ministers or nobles or independent people, but even if they encountered enlightened teachers, they would not believe them. They would be covetous and deluded and self-indulgent and would commit many bad deeds. Because of this bad karma, they would fall into the three mires. After countless eons, they might emerge from hell, only to be born poor and lowly. If they did not encounter an enlightened teacher, they would fall back into hell. They would go on transmigrating like this until now. All people are like this. This is called the path that is hard to travel. Thus the *Vimalakirti Sutra* says:

> It is impossible for people who cannot save themselves from their own illness to rescue other sick people.

The *Perfection of Wisdom Treatise* says:

Suppose there are two men. Each of them has a
relative drowning in a river. One man impetuously
plunges straight into the stream, without the power of
skill-in-means, so he and his relative both die. One
man has skill-in-means, so he goes and gets a boat and
rides it out to rescue his relative. Both he and his
relative escape drowning in the river. Bodhisattvas
who have first generated the aspiration for
enlightenment are like this too. If they have not
attained the power of forbearance, they are unable to
rescue sentient beings. Therefore they must constantly
be near to Buddha until they attain the forbearance [of
realizing that all phenomena] are unborn: only then
can they save sentient beings. It is like getting the boat
[in the parable].

The *Perfection of Wisdom Treatise* also says:

It is like a baby who must not leave his mother.
Otherwise he might fall into a well looking for milk to
drink and die. It is also like a baby bird whose wing
feathers have not yet fully formed. He must stay close
to the tree branch: he cannot venture far. Only after
his wing feathers have fully formed can he fly through
the sky free and unobstructed.


Ordinary people with no power can only concentrate
on reciting the name of Amitabha Buddha until they
achieve samadhi, stable concentration. When this work
is completed, then when they are about to die they can

gather in their thoughts and attain birth in the Pure Land and definitely get to see Amitabha Buddha.

After they have realized the forbearance that comes from knowing all things are unborn, then they can return to the Triple World: riding on the boat of forbearance, they can save suffering beings and serve buddha as they please independently. Therefore the *Perfection of Wisdom Treatise* says:

> Those who wander at play in hell are those who have been born in the Pure Land, attained forbearance toward unborn phenomena, and reentered the land of birth and death in order to convert hell beings and rescue suffering sentient beings.

For this reason, you should concentrate on cultivating Pure Land practice and vow to be born there. ...

## Yen-shou (Yung-ming) Advocates Pure Land

*Question*

[In Zen] we just see reality-nature and awaken to the Path, and immediately transcend birth and death. What is the use of tying the attention to Amitabha Buddha and seeking to be born in his land?

*Answer*

People who genuinely cultivate practice must examine themselves. It is like a person drinking water who knows for himself whether it is cold or warm. Now I will present some guidelines to break up the many forms of delusion.

Good people, you must observe yourselves. In your practice and your understanding, have you really managed to see reality-nature and awaken to the Path? Have you received the Tathagata's prediction of enlightenment and succeeded to the station of the patriarchs like Ashvaghosa and Nagarjuna? Have you attained unobstructed powers of argument and witnessed lotus flower samadhi like Chih-i of T'ien-t'ai? Have you mastered and practiced all the teachings of the Zen school like National Teacher Chung?

All these great beings understood the teachings imparted by Buddha and all of them urged people to be born in the Pure Land. In this they were benefitting both self and others. How could they have been misleading people and fooling themselves? Buddha himself praised [the Pure Land] and instructed people again and again [to seek to be born there]. I hope you will follow the virtuous ones of olden times and accept the Buddha's commands. They are surely not wrong. There are also the many clear stories of lofty people ancient and modern recorded in the Pure Land biographies. You should carefully read through them so that you may reflect on them.

You should also consider whether or not you are certain that you will be free to go or stay when you are about to die.

Are your sure that the barriers of evil karma from time without beginning will not appear before you?

Are you sure that this body of yours will escape from the cycle of birth and death?

Are you sure you can appear and disappear freely and without affliction on the evil paths of the three mires and nonhuman incarnations?

Are you sure there will be no impediment to your being born as you wish in the worlds of devas and humans?

If you are not sure, then do not make yourself sink down for eternal ages because of your temporary feeling of lofty self-satisfaction, and lose the advantages [of practicing Pure Land Buddhism]. ...

[Yung-ming's essay entitled] *Four Choices* says:

> First: Zen without Pure Land. Nine out of ten people take the wrong road here. If objects appear before them [as they meditate], they immediately follow them off.

This choice means that people only [strive to] illuminate reality-nature, and do not make vows to be born in the Pure Land. But as long as they flow along in this world "Endurance," there is the danger of falling back [into delusion] ...

> Second: Pure Land without Zen. Of ten thousand who practice [Pure Land Buddhism], ten thousand go [to the Pure Land]. They just get to see Amitabha Buddha: what worry is there that they won't be enlightened?

This choice means that they have not yet illuminated reality-nature, but they just vow to be born in the Pure

Land. Because they are riding upon the power of Buddha, they are sure to be free from doubt.

Third: Both Zen and Pure Land. This is like putting horns on a tiger [adding to its already formidable powers]. In this life these people will be teachers, and in lives to come they will be buddhas and patriarchs.

Since they profoundly comprehend the Buddha Dharma, they can be teachers to devas and humans. Moreover, they take vows to go to the Pure Land and ascend quickly to the stage from which there is no falling back ...

Fourth: Neither Zen nor Pure Land. This brings the torments of hell for ten thousand eons, with no one to rely on.

They do not understand the principles of Buddha, nor do they make vows to be born in the Pure Land. They sink down [into the sea of suffering] for eternal ages with no way to get out.

Good people, if you want to transcend birth and death, and experience enlightenment, choose well among these four options!

# This World and the Pure Land

Zen master Tsung-tse of Ch'ang-lu said:

Now let us compare this world "Endurance" with the Pure Land.

Here, birth in a flesh and blood body is painful. There, you are born by transformation in a lotus flower, and are free from the pains of birth.

Here, the seasons succeed each other and you weaken and grow old day by day. There, there are no hot and cold seasons, and you are free from the pains of aging.

Here, the physical body is hard to temper and often becomes sick. There, your transformed body is fragrant and pure and free from the pains of sickness.

Here, those who live to be seventy are rare and impermanence is swift. There, the lifespan is measureless and you are free from the pains of death.

Here, you fondly love those who are close to you, but you are sure to be separated from those you love. There, there are no parents or spouses or children, and you are free of the pain of being parted from loved ones.

Here, enemies hate you, and you are sure to be with those who resent you. There, those of the highest virtue are assembled together and you are free of the pain of being with those who hate you.

Here, you may be exhausted, and suffer from hunger and cold, and have unsatisfied cravings. There, food and clothing and precious things are provided ready-made for you to use.

Here, you may have a body that is ugly and defiled and has many defects. There, your countenance is dignified and your body shines with light.

Here, you revolve in the cycle of birth and death. There, you experience birthlessness.

Here, there are outcrops and depressions and brambles and thorns and the landscape is filled with filth and evil. There, the ground is made of gold, jewel trees reach to the sky, towers of precious stones rise up above you, and flowers of all colors are spread at your feet.

Here, Shakyamuni Buddha has already passed away and Maitreya Buddha has not yet come. There, Amitabha Buddha is preaching the Dharma right now.

Here, you look up in vain to the glory of Kuan-yin and Shih-chih. There, you are on intimate terms with these two bodhisattvas, and they are your special friends.

Here, a myriad of demons and heretics attempt to confuse correct cultivation. There, the Buddha's teaching unifies everything, and there is no trace of demons or heretics.

Here, lust misleads practitioners. There, your body is pure and clean, and there is no sexual desire.

Here, evil beasts and monsters beat their wings with an evil sound. There, the water birds and the forest trees all communicate the wondrous Dharma.

Comparing the two worlds, the landscape is as different as can be. The Pure Land is superior in countless ways: there is no time to mention them all.

Therefore all the scriptures of the complete meaning of the Great Vehicle point the way to the Pure Land.

The worthy sages of the past and present all make vows that they themselves and others will be born in the Pure Land.

Whoever wants to save people, must first recite the buddha-name himself or herself. Unfortunately, people do not think in long range terms: they only worry about things close at hand. Once the human body is lost, it is hard to regain it even in ten thousand eons. Thus I urge all sentient beings to recite "Amitabha Buddha" a hundred times or a thousand times or even ten thousand times [every day]. Transfer the merit to those who share the affinity [for the Pure Land], and vow to be born in Amitabha's land. ...

## Pure Land and Pure Mind

Layman Wang of Lung-shu said:

There are those in the world who specialize in studying Zen who say: "The Pure Land is mind-only: how could there be another pure land? Amitabha is inherent nature: it is not necessary to see another Amitabha."

This is all wrong. Why? These words are very lofty, but I am afraid it is very hard to reach the level [they indicate].

***

In the Pure Land in the west, there is no covetousness, no craving, no hatred, no ignorance. Can our minds be free of covetousness, craving, hatred, and ignorance?

In the Pure Land one has only to think of clothing and food, and receive them; one has only to think of being still or going, and one can be still or go. [Here on earth,] when our minds think of clothes, but we have no clothes, we are afflicted by cold. When our minds think of food, but we have no food, we are afflicted by hunger. When our minds want to be still, but we cannot be still, we are vexed by movement. When our minds want to go, but we cannot go, we are vexed by being tied down. So the Pure Land of mind-only which they talk about is really not easy to reach.

Amitabha Buddha is fully endowed with merit and wisdom. His supernatural powers are vast. He can change hell into a lotus flower land as easy as turning his hand over. He can observe infinite worlds right before his eyes.

For us, karmic barriers are serious, and we fear falling into hell: how can we change it into a lotus flower land? We cannot even see things on the other side of a wall, so how can we see infinite worlds? Thus it is really not easy to reach the level of the so-called Amitabha of inherent nature.

Those who study Zen must not ignore the Pure Land and not cultivate it; they must not abandon Amitabha and not wish to see him. The *Greater Amitabha Sutra* says:

In the ten directions there are countless bodhisattvas who go to the Pure Land.

If even these bodhisattvas want to be born in the Pure Land, who are we not to want to be born there? Are we better than the bodhisattvas?

Thus [the talk of] mind-only Pure Land and inherent nature Amitabha is high-sounding, but impractical. Those who practice without reaching [this level] mislead many people ...

It is better to walk on solid ground and cultivate practice by reciting the buddha-name. Then you can be born in the Pure Land directly and escape the cycle of birth and death straightaway. This is as far apart from the empty words without substance [of those who reject Pure Land Buddhism in favor of Zen] as heaven from earth.

*\*\**

Some say, "Certainly it is hard to see reality-nature by studying Zen. But what about studying [Taoism] to become an immortal?"

I respond: Not to cultivate the Pure Land and instead to want to study [Taoism] to become an immortal is like throwing away a fine jade that's in front of your eyes to seek an imitation jade that you cannot necessarily get. Isn't this a delusion?

Why so? According to the *Heroic March (Surangama) Sutra:*

There are ten kinds of immortals, who all live from a thousand to ten thousand years. But when their lifespans are exhausted, they again enter into the cycle of birth and death. Because they do not comprehend real nature, they are grouped with the six planes of sentient beings as the seventh level. They are all creatures in the cycle of birth and death.

When the people of the world study [Taoism] to become immortals, not one in ten thousand succeeds. Even if they do, they still do not avoid the cycle of birth and death, because they are attached to their bodies and their spirits, and cannot relinquish them. Body and spirit are false concepts that appear within true nature: they are not real. Therefore [Master] Han-shan's poem says:

> Even if you get to be an immortal,
> It is just like holding onto a dead man's ghost;
> It is not as good as the Buddhists
> Who are unconstrained by birth and death.

## Pointing the Way to the Pure Land

Enlightened teachers who have pointed the way to the Pure Land are numerous as atoms of dust. Here I will briefly quote some of them to offer their testimony.

Master T'ien-ju said:

I often see those who study Zen these days but do not investigate the final meaning of the Tathagata [in the sutras] and do not know the mystic device of Bodhidharma [in Zen]. With empty bellies and proud hearts, they study how to be crazy and false. When they see people who cultivate the Pure Land, they laugh at them and say, "That study is done by ignorant men and women. How vulgar!"

I say that it is not [only] ignorant men and women whom they are calling vulgar. [In fact] they are calling vulgar [some of the greatest figures in Buddhist lore, who also sanctioned Pure Land practice, like] Manjushri and Samantabhadra, Ashvaghosa and Nagarjuna, and so on.

This type [who reject Pure Land as vulgar] are not only deluded themselves about the correct path; they are cutting off the seed of enlightenment within themselves and creating the [bad] karma of slandering the Dharma. They are also bringing upon themselves the disaster that comes from denigrating the sages. Can we not warn them?

By the other methods, it is hard to escape birth and death. By cultivating buddha-remembrance through recitation of the buddha-name it is easy to be liberated from the cycle of birth and death. [Shakyamuni Buddha] left us the name of Amitabha Buddha to rescue sentient beings. Those who do not believe in it and who slander it will surely fall into hell and suffer all kinds of pain.

Dharma Teacher Ling-chih said:

The ordinary people who fill the earth are bound by karma and delusion and revolve in the five planes of existence, subject to all kinds of pain and affliction for thousands and thousands of eons. Suddenly they hear of the Pure Land and aspire to seek birth there: one day they invoke the buddha-name and immediately transcend the world. This can be called something that is hard to encounter in ten thousand ages, something that is met with once in a thousand births.

If people are willing to recite "Amitabha Buddha," this surpasses all the roots of goodness. Even if they are able to practice giving and uphold discipline and meditate and chant the sutras, these practices are not as meritorious as reciting the buddha-name. Why? If they cultivate all sorts of meritorious karma, without correct faith to seek birth in the Pure Land, these are all minor roots of goodness. To recite "Amitabha Buddha" and vow to seek birth in the Pure Land is called the great root of goodness.

## Dharma Teacher Ku-shan said:

To seek birth in the Pure Land is to depend on "other power": Amitabha's vows gather you in, Shakyamuni encourages and praises you, and all the buddhas protect you and are mindful of you. All three [kinds of 'other power'] are present.

If you have the mind of faith, being born in the Pure Land is extremely easy. It is like crossing the sea when you already have a great ship, a skillful pilot, and a favorable wind: you are sure to arrive quickly on the other shore. If you do not consent to board the boat, and hesitate and tarry on dangerous paths, whose fault is this?

## Legal Supervisor Yang said:

Among the buddhas, Shakyamuni was the great guide and teacher: he pointed out the Pure Land, the Land of

Peace and Bliss. Amitabha is the teacher of the Pure Land. If sentient beings are born in that land, they are free from suffering.

Those who have not heard of the Pure Land are certainly to be pitied. Especially to be lamented are those good people who develop the attitude that they will not seek birth in the Pure Land. One group says, "We must go beyond the buddhas and patriarchs; the Pure Land is not worth being born in." A second group says, "The Pure Land is everywhere; it is not necessary to be born in the west." A third group says, "The Pure Land is a holy realm; we are ordinary people and cannot be born there."

Now Samantabhadra, with his ocean of practices beyond measure, vowed to see the land of Amitabha Buddha. Vimalakirti always cultivated the Pure Land. All the Tathagatas of the ten directions praised the Pure Land. All the bodhisattvas of the ten directions had the same intent to go to the Pure Land. Try to decide for yourself: how do you compare with these sages? If you think that the Pure Land is not worth being born in, how you are deceiving yourself!

In the *Lankavatara Sutra* there is the prediction that the ancestral teacher Lung Meng [would be born in the Pure Land]. Ashvaghosa, the great philosopher, in his *Treatise on the Immeasurable*, had a verse on seeking birth in the Pure Land. Tz'u-en began his eulogies by acclaiming the ten excellences [of the Pure Land]. [The T'ien-t'ai Patriarch] Chih-i analyzed the principles [of the Pure Land] clearly in his *Treatise on the Ten Doubts*. All these great sages enthusiastically progressed towards the Pure Land. If you think it is not necessary to be born in the Pure Land, how arrogant you are being!

A burning cart can be destroyed, but a boat filled with stones does not sink. [Even the greatest sinners] have been reborn in the Pure Land. The transgressions of worldly people cannot be compared to them. If you think you cannot be born in the Pure Land, how you are abandoning yourself!

## Zen master Chung-feng said:

Our world "Endurance" is painful. Who can count its sufferings? But worldly people think suffering is happiness and willingly dwell in it. Many lose their place. They emerge from a stinking bag of skin,[42] to constantly nurture their disease of ignorance until it becomes a fetid poison. Suddenly the vital energy in their hearts dissipates and they die. They turn into cold ashes and are buried underground. They flow on in the five planes of existence without a moment's rest. For a hundred eons, through a thousand births, they endure bitter pain.

Good people, wouldn't it be better to start right away to recite Amitabha's name and abandon the sufferings of this world?

The bliss of the Western Paradise: who can awaken to it? The people and the land are all of special excellence. There is no cold or hot season. There is no evil. The people there emerge from a lotus flower womb to listen to the sound of the Dharma and celestial music. The crystalline ground sparkles with light: there is no trace of dust. There are towers made of gold and silver and pearls and jewels. Splendid food and clothing appears spontaneously by magic. The lifespan is measureless, incalculable.

Good people, wouldn't it be better to start to recite Amitabha's name right away and gain the bliss of the Western Paradise?

## Vinaya Master Pien-hsiu said:

I specialize in the vinaya, the codes of monastic conduct, and I recite the buddha-name. I consider the Pure Land as the refuge of peaceful nurturance.

People who have not fully comprehended the Zen school sometimes say that reciting the buddha-name is a provisional method, a minor teaching; sometimes they say that it is a formalistic version of the Great Vehicle. This is twisted talk by confused minds; it is not a penetrating comment that is lofty and illuminated. Why? [On the absolute level] whatever is uttered is reality-nature and whatever is thought is thusness; all forms and all scents are the Middle Path. How much the more so, for my correct mindfulness [engendered by reciting the buddha-name]!

## Zen Master Chen-hsieh Liao said:

The only quick shortcut method is reciting the buddha-name. Reciting the buddha-name is the most effective and is the easiest to make progress in. If you seek to escape [from birth and death] without reciting the buddha-name, you will never get anywhere. I urge everyone to recite the buddha-name with pure faith and a unified mind, and vow to seek birth in the Pure Land. You certainly won't go wrong.

Zen Master Ku-yin said:

The phrase "Amitabha Buddha" is the first meditation case of the Zen school. It is like a staff to help you mount a horse. It is a means to hold fast to the living shore.

No matter whether monks or nuns or laymen or laywomen recite it, they all will get results. In their present life they will increase their good fortune and dispel disaster, and for future lives they will forever remove all bad karma. If people recite it right where they are, everything will go as they wish and their hopes will be fulfilled. They will be fortunate enough to be reborn in the central land as human beings.

[Living a human life] is like ascending a mountain of jewels: you must not go in vain and return in vain. [Reciting the buddha-name] is an urgent duty: you should take care of it soon.

Yama the King of Death does not value gold and jewels: all that impresses him is the phrase "Amitabha Buddha." A lifetime of wealth and high rank passes like the clouds. A hundred years of time is as brief as a flash of lightning. Those who know the sound of the Dharma must not delay. You must make the transformation soon. Buddha is the ship for the ocean of suffering. You should cross over to the other shore **soon.**

First, it is most important to maintain a vegetarian diet and uphold the precepts.

Second, you must change your bad habits and go toward virtue.

Third, you need enlightened teachers and spiritual friends.

Fourth, you need correct vows to be liberated.

Fifth, you must recognize cause and effect.

Sixth, you must have skillful means.

Seventh, you must accumulate merit and virtue.

Eighth, you must increase your meritorious affinities.

Whether you are walking, standing, sitting, or lying down, you must recite the phrase "Amitabha Buddha" without a break. You must believe that if the causal basis is profound, the result will be profound.

Do not pay attention to your own thoughts. If you can go from moment to moment [mindful of buddha], I guarantee that your mindfulness will become unified. If as you are mindful [of buddha] you can recognize the person who is mindful, Amitabha appears together with you, and you enter the samadhi of buddha-name recitation. You personally experience the inner court of ultimate bliss, and your name is inscribed on a lotus womb [from which you will be in Amitabha's Pure Land].

Those with the highest accomplishment see themselves
and see Amitabha up close. They receive his prediction
of enlightenment, and as companions of the
bodhisattvas [in the Pure Land] continue on to supreme
enlightenment.

## Layman Wu-chin said:

I lament for those whose bodies dwell in the world of
form, and whose minds take pleasure in the emptiness.
I consider that in this world the five corruptions
confuse their minds and the multitude of evils mix with
their natures. Since they lack the power of correct
contemplation, and do not have the power to
comprehend causes, they cannot awaken to the
Amitabha of inherent nature and the Pure Land of
mind-only.

People should carefully follow the teachings from the
golden mouth of the World Honored One Shakyamuni
and concentrate their thoughts on Amitabha Buddha
and his Paradise in the west. They should seek the
protection of the great power of Amitabha's great
vows. Then when this lifetime is over, going to be
born in the land of ultimate bliss will be as easy as
riding a boat with the current: they will arrive without
exerting their own strength.

## Pure Land Patriarch Hui-yuan said:

People in the Zen school see people reciting the
buddha-name and cultivating the Pure Land and they
all say that this is cultivating practice with attachment
to form, that this is not to be considered subtle and

wondrous, and is not as good as seeing reality-nature
and suddenly awakening to eternal reality by studying
Zen.

Those of shallow faculties believe this confused idea.
They do not recite the buddha-name, and they do not
read the scriptures: in the midst of lives devoted to
serving the senses, they give lip service to studying Zen.
Their minds do not practice the Path, but they
denigrate the Pure Land and do not believe in birth
there.

This is a great mistake. They do not realize that
Amitabha Buddha is the highest most profound Zen.
These people have not plumbed the great true
principle, and so they falsely differentiate [between Zen
and Pure Land].

If you want to study Zen and see reality-nature, it is
not necessary to take up any other meditation topic:
just recite the phrase "Amitabha Buddha." Study it,
recite it, investigate it, doubt it. After a long time, you
will have some attainment. Even if you do not awaken
at this time, when your life is over, you will be born in
the highest class in the Pure Land. [Once you are born
there] what worry is there that you will not achieve
great enlightenment?

\*\*\*

Take the example of Zen Master Pai-chang Huai-hai.
He was the true heir to whom Ma-tsu of Chiang-tzu
transmitted the Dharma. All the Zen communities in
the country have followed the precedents he

established, and from ancient times until now no one
has dared to suggest that he was wrong. The "Pure
Rules" for monastic communities all over China are
based on his standards, and from start to finish, no one
has dared to transgress against his teaching on any
point.

We observe that Pai-chang's guidelines for chanting on
behalf of a sick monk say: "Gather together the
congregation and join in reciting a verse praising
Amitabha Buddha. Then all together chant 'Hail to
Amitabha Buddha' a hundred or a thousand times.
Dedicate the merit [to the sick monk] and express this
humble hope: 'If his causal connections are not yet
ended, may he quickly recover. If his fate is impossible
to escape, may he quickly ascend to the Pure Land.'"
Isn't Pai-chang pointing the way to the Pure Land?

We also observe Pai-chang's guidelines for seeing off a
dead monk. "At night chant the sutras and dedicate
the merit [to the dead man]. Humbly express this
wish: 'May his spirit quickly rise to the realm of
purity and may his karma leave behind the afflictions
of the sense-objects. May the lotus open out a flower
of the highest class [for him to be born in] and may the
Buddha give him a prediction of enlightenment in one
lifetime.'" Isn't this pointing the way to the Pure
Land?

At the time of cremation, the duty distributor is
directed to lead in ten repetitions of a loud chant of
"Hail to the Land of Ultimate Bliss in the west and to
the great compassionate Amitabha Buddha." The
whole congregation joins in. The whole thing is called

the ten invocations. After the chanting is finished, the merit is transferred [to the dead monk] and [the duty distributor] says, "These ten invocations we have just made are to help [the dead man] go to the Pure Land." Isn't this pointing the way to the Pure Land?

Ever since Pai-chang, wherever they have a funeral for a dead monk, they always follow this model. Thus it may be said that all the Five Houses of Zen, and all the Zen monks in the country, all return to the Pure Land.

I observe that the words of the adepts all point the way to the Pure Land. When today's Zen students falsely claim that enlightened people do not vow to be born in the Pure Land, they do not understand the intent of the Zen masters, and they themselves have no insight or awakening. They will not escape regretting this later.

## Pure Land references in the scriptures

Pure Land scriptures are as numerous as the sands of the Ganges. Here I quote a few in brief in order to dispel doubts.

The *Sutra of Infinite Life (Longer Amitabha Sutra)* says:

[Shakyamuni] Buddha told Maitreya: "In this world there are seventy-two billion bodhisattvas beyond the stage of falling back who will go to be born in the Land of Ultimate Bliss. Countless numbers of bodhisattvas of minor practice will all be born there. Not only in my land, but in all the worlds of the ten directions, countless multitudes of great bodhisattvas recite the name of Amitabha Buddha and vow to be born in Amitabha Buddha's land."

The *Amitabha Sutra* says:

If good men and good women hear of Amitabha Buddha and recite his name, because they invoke his name, all their bad karma will dissolve away. When these people are about to die, they will immediately go to be born in Amitabha Buddha's Land of Ultimate Bliss.

Shakyamuni Buddha said, "All of you should believe what I say and what all the buddhas say. If sentient beings hear this, they should vow to be born in the Pure Land."

The *Sixteen Contemplations of Amitabha Sutra (Meditation Sutras* says:

If good men and good women simply hear the name of Amitabha Buddha and the names of the two bodhisattvas [who accompany him, Kuan-yin and Shih-chih], it removes the sins of countless eons of birth and death. This is even more true if they keep them in mind. One repetition of "Hail to Amitabha Buddha" wipes away the serious bad karma of eight billions eons of birth and death.

You must realize that those who recite the buddha-name are rare flowers among humans, and that the bodhisattvas Kuan-yin and Shih-chih are their excellent friends.

In the *Lotus Sutra* chapter entitled "The Fundamental Mission of the Medicine King Bodhisattva" it says:

> If you hear this sutra and practice according to what it teaches, then at the end of this life you will go to the Land of Peaceful Bliss and your abode will be surrounded by Amitabha Buddha and a multitude of great bodhisattvas. You will be reborn in a lotus flower on a jewel throne. No more will you be afflicted by desire, by anger, by ignorance, by arrogance and jealousy, or by any other defilements. You will attain the supernatural powers of the bodhisattvas and the infinite forbearance that comes from recognizing that all phenomena are unborn (tolerance of no-birth).

The *Perfection of Wisdom Treatise* says:

> Buddha is the supreme Dharma King. The great bodhisattvas are ministers to the Dharma. The one the ministers honor is Buddha, the Dharma King.

> The bodhisattvas think to themselves: "In the past we slandered transcendent wisdom and fell into evil paths. We received measureless suffering for countless ages. Even though we cultivated other practices, we were unable to emerge from the sea of suffering. Later we met enlightened teachers who taught us to recite 'Amitabha Buddha' and we managed to wipe away the barriers of bad karma and be born in the Pure Land. Now we must give thanks to Amitabha Buddha. Why

so? Our parents and friends and the kings of humans and devas could not save us and bring us out of the sea of suffering. We escaped from the sea of suffering only because of the protection of the power of the vows of Amitabha Buddha." ...

The *Precious Mirror of the Lotus School* says:

Of the countless multitude of Tathagatas, Amitabha is foremost. Of the innumerable buddha-lands in the ten directions, the Pure Land is the refuge. We must have deep faith that the Pure Land is the wondrous gate of true liberation. We must truly consider that Amitabha is the real compassionate father of sentient beings.

Therefore, when mindfulness [of buddha] arises, the myriad luminous beings know. When the mind of faith is born, all the buddhas appear. As soon as we invoke the precious name [of Amitabha], we have already planted a seed in the lotus womb [in the Pure Land]. Once we generate enlightenment, our names are inscribed in the golden land.

If you have an affinity and encounter this teaching, then you will awaken and cultivate it. If your faith is shallow and you do not recite [the buddha-name], then you are very foolish and very wrong.

How lamentable! It is the last age and there are many misguided views. The deluded castigate Pure Land Buddhism as a provisional vehicle, and criticize reciting the buddha-name as a crude practice. Thus they sink down into the burning house and willingly accept endless ages of being submerged [in birth and death]. They go against their compassionate father [Amitabha] and suffer the deep pain of passing a lifetime in vain.

You must believe that unless you rely on the power of Amitabha, you will have no way to cut off karmic delusion. If you do not encounter this teaching, you will have no way to escape from birth and death.

Thus, those who despise Pure Land Buddhism are despising themselves, and those who attack it are attacking themselves. False sentiments are easy to learn; the correct Dharma is hard to hear of. If you go on and on revolving in the three evil planes of existence, you will never manage to get out.

The *Essential Gate for Contemplating the Pure Land* says:

The Pure Land teaching is, for sentient beings in the last age, the essential road out of birth and death and the boat to cut across the ocean of birth and death.

Once they are born there, beings never fall back. With gold-colored bodies, they fly free. Food and clothing are received spontaneously. They see [Amitabha] Buddha and hear the Dharma and quickly enter the ranks of the sages ... They are not tormented by thunder and wind and rain and cold and heat or harried by hunger and thirst. They are born by transformation in the lotus flower, and their lifespans are immeasurable. They are free from the pains of birth, old age, sickness, and death. Thus it is the world of ultimate bliss.

Therefore our Tathagata Shakyamuni opened the door
[to the Pure Land], so as to enable deluded sentient
beings in this world to escape from the multitude of
sufferings here. Amitabha, our compassionate father,
showed the road to his protection. Thus they
repeatedly instructed us and emphatically praised the
Pure Land, and urged us all to be born there.

Because of this, the worthy sages and clergy and
laypeople who have recited the buddha-name and have
gone to the Pure Land have been too numerous to
count.

How painful it is when low grade ordinary people are
attached to sensory afflictions and do not seek to leave
them behind, and willingly flow on in birth and death!

The *Peace and Bliss Collection* says:

If you can recite the name of Amitabha Buddha, you
immediately cut off all karmic obstructions, and you
will get to be born in the Pure Land.

Why so? It is like a man who uses lion's sinews for
the strings on his zither: once they sound, all other
strings break. If a person with the mind of
enlightenment can recite "Amitabha Buddha," the
heavy barriers of affliction are all broken and
destroyed. It is also like a man who puts a drop of
lion's milk into a bowl filled with the milk of cows,
goats, donkeys and horses: all these types of milk turn
to water. If a person within the mind of enlightenment
can recite "Amitabha Buddha," all the barriers of evil

delusion spontaneously dissolve, and he or she gets to
be born in the Pure Land.

The *Treatise to Resolve Doubts* says:

It is hard to obtain a human body, but it is easy to be
born in the Pure Land. What is the reason?

If you do not uphold the five precepts, then the road
of devas and humans is cut off. You get to be a human
only if you uphold the five precepts. Because the five
precepts are difficult to uphold, and you have no power
of vows to protect you, a human body is hard to
obtain.

When you cultivate the Pure Land, it is not necessary
to uphold the five precepts perfectly. Just recite the
name of Amitabha Buddha. Even if you have bad
karma, you are permitted to repent. When you are
about to die, Amitabha Buddha and Kuan-yin and Shih-
chih and an oceanic assembly of pure beings each with
the power of vows will come together to receive you
and protect you. Thus it is easy to be born in the Pure
Land.

The *Dharma Gate of Pure Practice* says:

Repentance is like carefully polishing an ancient mirror
to remove the obscuring dust that has accumulated
through the ages. Reciting the buddha-name is like
having a private audience with an enlightened lord, and
securing his timely aid.

Spring, summer, fall, and winter, while walking, standing, sitting, and lying down, carefully contemplate the adornments of the Pure Land, and always be mindful of Amitabha Buddha. If you recite the buddha-name like this, then samadhi will appear before you, and you will be born in the Pure Land. There is no need to doubt this.

The *Moon Treasury Scripture* says:

In the last age of the Dharma, billions and billions of sentient beings practice and cultivate the Path, but scarcely one succeeds. This is because it is hard to succeed in the various schools, in the evil world of the five corruptions. The Pure Land gate is the only way to enter.

You must realize that your own practice is hard to perfect, but it is easy to arrive through the "other power" [of Amitabha]. It is like a lowly man who adheres to the power of a universal monarch, and so can fly all over the world. It is like an ordinary mortal who relies on the efficacy of the medicine of the immortals, and who ascends to the abode of the immortals. It is really an easy path, and you must hasten to get into accord with it. Inscribe this compassionate method on your bones.

The *Great Perfection of Wisdom Sutra* says:

If a person recites the buddha-name with a scattered mind, she will still get away from suffering: the merit [of buddha-name recitation] does not end. How much the more so, if one recites the buddha-name with fixed attention.    [The effectiveness of reciting the buddha-name] extends from [reciting it with] mind unified and undisturbed to [deathbed] recitation ten times.

The *Lotus Sutra* says:

If a person with his mind scattered and confused enters a shrine and chants "Hail to Buddha," he has already achieved the Buddha Path.

The buddha-name is heard through the ten directions and brings vast benefits to sentient beings.  It contains all the roots of goodness and helps promote the supreme mind [of enlightenment].

The *Flower Ornament (Avatamsaka) Sutra* says:

Whatever you are doing, always be mindful of the merits of Buddha, day and night without interruption. You must act like this.

Better to endure the sufferings of hell and hear the names of the buddhas than to receive all kinds of bliss and not hear the names of the buddhas.

The *Jewel Heap Sutra* says:

When the beings of other regions hear the name of the Tathagata Amitabha, they are able to generate pure faith and joyously accept all the roots of goodness. They transfer their merit [to the Pure Land] and vow to be born in Amitabha's land.  According to their vows, they are born there, and never turn back until they achieve buddhahood.

# Pure Land Visions

The T'ang period monk Hui-jih [resided in] the Wang-chi Temple in Lo-yang. His lay surname was Hsin, and he was from Tung-lai. During the reign of Emperor Chung-tsung [705-709] he was ordained. After he had received the precepts in full, he met I-ching San-tsang, who had studied the ultimate mysteries of the One Vehicle and who had journeyed to India. Hui-jih always felt great respect for I-ching, so he vowed to visit the western regions too.

Hui-jih set out by ship and crossed the sea. In three years he visited all the countries in the Southeastern Sea. After passing through them all, he arrived in India. He went to pay his respects to the holy sites where Shakyamuni Buddha had preached. He also sought out Buddhist texts in Sanskrit. For thirteen years he called on men of knowledge and asked them to instruct him in the Dharma.

Wanting to benefit others [with what he had learned], Hui-jih journeyed back to his homeland. He travelled alone across the snowy mountains and the lands of the barbarians for four years. He had endured many hardships, and he had grown profoundly weary with this world.

He sighed to himself saying, "In what land, in what region, is there happiness without suffering? By what method, by what practice, can we quickly see Buddha?"

All over India he had questioned men learned in the Buddhist Canon, and they had all extolled the Pure Land. Moreover, this was in accord with what Buddha had said. As for its quickness, [they told him], it is a road [that can be travelled] in a single lifetime; when this body is used up, you are sure to attain birth in the world of ultimate bliss, and serve Amitabha Buddha in person. When Hui-jih heard this, he humbly accepted it.

During the course of his travels, he came to North India. Northeast of the royal city of the land of Gandhara, there was a large mountain where there was a statue of Kuan-yin. Kuan-yin often appeared there to those who prayed to her sincerely.

Hui-jih had earnestly beseeched her for seven days without eating, and was ready to go on like that until death. On the night of the seventh day, before midnight, Kuan-yin appeared in the sky in a purple and gold body ten feet high sitting on a jewel lotus.

She reached down and rubbed the top of Hui-jih's head and said to him, "You want to transmit the Dharma to benefit yourself and others. There is the land of Amitabha Buddha in the west. Urge people to recite the buddha-name, chant the scriptures, and vow to be born there. When they reach that land, they will see Amitabha Buddha and me, and obtain great benefits. You must realize that the Pure Land teaching is superior to all other practices." After she finished speaking, she suddenly disappeared.

Hui-jih was tired from having gone without food, but when he heard this, his strength came back. He set off across the mountains to return to the east [to China]. He travelled through more than seventy lands, and was away eighteen years altogether.

In 719 he finally arrived in [the Chinese capital] Ch'ang-an. He had an audience with the Emperor and presented him with the images of buddha and the sacred texts that he had brought from India, to enlighten the Emperor's mind. [The Emperor was pleased] and bestowed on him the title Dharma Master Tz'u-min San-tsang.

Thereafter Hui-jih always scrupulously cultivated Pure Land practice. He wrote a collection of stories about birth in the Pure Land which circulated throughout the country. His path was the same teaching as that of [the Pure Land pioneers] Shan-tao and Shao-k'ang, but in a different time.

\*\*\*

In 767, during the T'ang period, the great teacher Fa-chao was staying at Yun-feng Temple in Hang-chou. He was scrupulous in his practice and never slackened. He took it as his urgent duty to urge people to recite the buddha-name.

[One day] in the monks' hall, [a vision] appeared twice in the big pot in which the gruel was cooked. A holy site on Mount Wu-t'ai appeared, with a temple with a golden signboard that said "Manjushri's Bamboo Forest Temple."

After this, Fa-chao felt a longing to pay homage on Mount Wu-t'ai. At Hu-tung Temple in Hang-chou he built five worship halls where people met to recite the buddha-name. He vowed to see Manjushri.

On the thirteenth day of the eight month of 769, Fa-chao set out for Mount Wu-t'ai, and on the fifth day of the fourth month of 770 he arrived in Wu-t'ai county. From far off he saw several rays of white light on the south side of Buddha Light Temple. The next day he arrived at Buddha Light Temple and it was identical to what he had seen in the vision in the pot.

That night after midnight, Fa-chao saw a ray of light come down from north of the mountain. It shined on him, and he rushed into the hall and asked the congregation of monks, "What omen is this? Is it lucky or unlucky?"

There was a monk who answered, "This is Manjushri's inconceivable light: it always shines on those who have an affinity with him."

When he heard this, moving with full solemnity, Fa-chao immediately went to follow the light.

Fa-chao went about fifteen miles northeast from the temple, and there was a mountain there. At the foot of the mountain was a brook, and on the north side of the brook there was a stone gate.

There were two boys about eight years old dressed in dark blue clothes standing at the gate with solemn expressions on their faces. One was called Shan-tsai and one was called Nan-ta. When they saw Fa-chao they happily asked him how he was and bowed. Then they led him through the gate. After the three of them had walked about two miles, there appeared a tower with a golden gate. As they gradually came up to the gate, they saw it was a temple. In front of the temple was a large gold signboard that said, "Manjushri's Bamboo Forest Temple," just as in the vision Fa-chao had originally seen in the pot of boiling gruel.

The temple complex was about six miles in circumference, and contained a hundred and twenty buildings. There were jewel stupas and the grounds were decorated with pure gold. It was filled with flowing streams and flowering trees.

Fa-chao entered the temple and went into the lecture hall. There he saw Manjushri on the west and Samantabhadra on the east, each seated on a lion throne. He could hear the sound of their voices expounding the Dharma very clearly. Around Manjushri were more than ten thousand bodhisattvas. Samantabhadra was also surrounded by countless bodhisattvas.

Fa-chao went before the two great bodhisattvas, bowed in homage, and asked them: "Ordinary people in the last age are far from the time of the sages. Teachers are of progressively lower quality, and the obstructions of defilement are ever thicker. People have no way to manifest their buddha-nature. The Buddha Dharma grows vague and indistinct. I do not know what method to practice, what method is the most essential. I hope you great sages will cut my net of doubts."

Manjushri replied: "You recite the buddha-name. None of the practices of the time surpasses reciting the buddha-name, supporting the Buddha, Dharma, and

Sangha, and cultivating merit and wisdom. This is the most direct most essential method.

"What is the reason? I attained omniscience because in ages past I contemplated buddha, recited the buddha-name, and supported the Buddha, Dharma, and Sangha. All the phenomena of enlightenment, from the perfection of wisdom, to meditative concentration, to Buddhahood, are all born from reciting the buddha-name. Thus we know that reciting the buddha-name is the king of all the dharmas. You must constantly be mindful of [Buddha], the Supreme Dharma King, and never stop."

Fa-chao also asked: "How should we be mindful of Buddha?"

Manjushri said: "To the west of this world is Amitabha Buddha. The power of his vows is inconceivable. You should constantly recite his name without a break. Then at the end of your life, you are sure to be born in his land and never fall back."

After Manjushri had said this, both great bodhisattvas extended their golden hands and rubbed the top of Fa-chao's head and gave him a prediction of enlightenment.

Then they bade him farewell and said, "Since you have already been reciting the buddha-name, it will not be long before you experience supreme correct enlightenment. If good men and good women wish to become buddhas quickly, nothing is better than reciting the buddha-name. Then they will be able to experience supreme enlightenment quickly."

When their words were finished, the two great sages spoke verses to each other. When Fa-chao heard them, he was leaping with joy, and his doubts were all removed. He again bowed in homage, gave thanks, and withdrew.

# All Practices are Unified in Buddha-Remembrance

Zen Master Wan-tsung said:

The samadhi of reciting the buddha-name is called one-practice samadhi.

This is because the people who practice it comprehend its profound intent and are able to uphold it singlemindedly without becoming involved with other practices, so they are only mindful of the Pure Land, and only remember Amitabha Buddha. They know that Amitabha's body and the Pure Land are not two, and mindfulness of the Pure Land and remembrance of Amitabha are one. Hence the name "one-practice."

Nevertheless, though it is called one-practice, those who practice it also must use as aids in the Path all the countless worldly and world-transcending dharmas, and all the meritorious practices, and thus proceed quickly to be born in the Pure Land.

Therefore all practices are Pure Land, and no divergent roads are cultivated. It is called unified practice. This can be compared to the myriad streams which all flow into the sea, and all get the the same name, "the sea." The myriad virtues all return together and get the name "one-practice." Thus all forms of mindfulness, correct effort, and awakening to the Path, the four great vows [to bring universal salvation], and the six perfections (paramitas) [of bodhisattvas] are all Pure Land practices ...


## Revealing True Nature Apart from Form: Women go to the Pure Land


*Question:*

Can women recite the buddha-name and get to be born in the Pure Land or not?

*Answer:*

What kind of talk is this? Even the birds can get to be born in the Pure Land by reciting the buddha-name.[43] This is even more true of human beings.

*Objection:*

But a woman's body has ten evils, so how can they get to be born in the Pure Land?

First, when she is born, her parents are not happy. Second, when they raise her, they do so without interest. Third, [a girl is taught] always to be fearful of people. Fourth, her parents worry about arranging a marriage for her. Fifth, she leaves her parents [to live with her husband's family]. Sixth, she lives in fear of her husband's moods. Seventh, pregnancy and childbirth are very difficult. Eighth, when she is young, she is tightly controlled by her parents. Ninth, when she is grown up, she is ruled by her husband. Tenth, when she gets old, she is scolded by her sons and grandsons. From birth to death, she is never free. ...

So how can a woman quickly become enlightened?

*Answer:*

These [disadvantages] exist if we talk about the level of external forms, but if we talk about inherent nature, none of these things exist.

At one time, a naga girl barely eight years old who had sharp faculties of wisdom became enlightened in an instant. How could this be a matter of male and female, or old and young? In the assemblies of the Zen schools, many women have illuminated mind, seen reality-nature, and become buddhas and enlightened teachers in their current lifetimes, and even more have done so in future lifetimes.

If you cling to the idea that physical form is real, you utterly fail to comprehend the inner truth of reality-nature. You do not understand it, but when men and women merge with the source of reality-nature, they are neither male nor female. ...

Haven't you read the *Source Mirror?* It says:

The physical body appears to have the characteristics of birth and death and male and female, but the inherent identity, which is luminous and aware, really does not have these characteristics. If you awaken to this inherent identity right now, this is called eternal life, the lifespan of the Tathagatas, and the wondrous mind of nirvana.

It also says:

> Whatever has mind becomes buddha. Right now your
> walking is buddha walking, and your sitting is buddha
> sitting. Thus it is said that all physical embodiments
> and environments are entirely situated within the most
> holy inherent mind, and that the body of reality of all
> the buddhas is not apart from the thoughts of the
> lowest ordinary people.

[The Zen adept] Prime Minister P'ei Hsiu said:

> Whatever has blood and breath is sure to have
> awareness. Whatever has awareness must share the same
> essence [as the buddhas].

Just as it is said [by all Buddhist authorities], all
sentient beings, even the insects, have buddha-nature.
This certainly includes women!

*Question:*
   Since they possess buddha-nature, why don't insects
become buddhas? Why do they remain in the cycle of
birth and death subject to suffering instead?

*Answer:*
   It is just because they are attached to form and
deluded about reality nature: they turn their backs on
enlightenment and join with the dusts of sensory
experience and create all kinds of evil karma, so they fall
into non- human levels and suffer. But let us put aside
the case of insects for now and say no more about it.

Right now you have gotten a human body, but you are still unwilling to maintain a vegetarian diet, uphold the precepts, recite the buddha-name, and seek birth in the Pure Land. Instead, you want to make the non-human species become buddhas.

*Question:*

Often when teachers see a woman who is a vegetarian and upholds the precepts and recites the buddha-name, they will express their wish that she may turn into a man in future lifetimes in order to cultivate the Path. What about such talk?

*Answer:*

This type loudly lays claim to the name "teacher," but they do not comprehend the inner truth of being an enlightened teacher. In reality they are ignorant and deluded. Don't they know [this story] from the *Vimalakirti Sutra?*

Shariputra said to a female deva, "Why don't you transform your woman's body [and turn into a man]?"

The devi said, "For eleven years I looked for the marks of a woman's body, but in the end they could not be found. What is there to transform? Suppose a magician conjured up an apparition of a woman. If someone asked, 'Why don't you transform this woman's body [into a man]?' would this be a correct question?"

Shariputra said, "No. A magical apparition has no fixed form, so what is there to transform?"

The devi said, "All phenomena are also like this: they

do not have fixed form. So why do you ask me why I do not transform my woman's body?"

In an instant, the devi used her supernatural powers to transform Shariptura so he looked like her, and transform herself so she looked like him. Then she asked him, "Why don't you transform your woman's body?"

Shariputra, in the form of a female deva, answered, "Now I do not know what transformation has changed my body into a woman's body."

The devi said, "Shariputra, if you were able to transform this woman's body, then all women would also be able to transform their own bodies. You are not a woman, but you appear in a woman's body. All women are also like this. Though they appear with women's bodies, they are not [in essence] women. Therefore Buddha said that all phenomena are neither male nor female."

Then the devi drew back her supernatural powers, and Shariputra returned to the way he was before.

Thus, in the inherent nature of true thusness, how could there be the characteristics "male" and "female"? Moreover, in the Lotus Sutra it specifically predicts that women will be born in the Land of Ultimate Bliss. How could it not be so? Furthermore, the Pure Land biographies record countless numbers of women who have been born in the Western Paradise. How could an genuine enlightened teacher not know this?

# A Real Buddhist Life

Master T'ien-ju said:

In recent generations there have been those who leave home and say that they have left behind worldly life, but who have not cleared away their conventional habits. They say they have left the sensory dusts, but they have not cut their ties to sense objects.

They certainly do not know the teachings of the scriptures, and they do not know how to study Zen. In them the mind-monkey is still running around in confusion, and the thought-horse is still charging onward.

They form groups and pass their days arguing. Not only do they consume the offerings of the faithful in vain; they also bury their own luminous awareness. When the light falls from their eyes [and they are about to die], where will the road lead? ...

If you claim realization when you have not experienced realization, and claim attainment before you have attained anything, then you have entered the Zen school in vain, and you will go on being born and dying to no avail.

Alas! I ask you: why did you leave home? For the sake of food and clothing? Because you craved riches and high rank? To look for security and happiness? Did your parents give you up to become a monk hoping that you would save them? Or did you leave home to repay the fourfold benevolence of your parents, your ruler, your teachers, and the buddhas?

Now you do not even have anything to rely on yourselves, so how can you save other people? Someday old Yama [the judge of the dead] will demand an accounting from you for the money you spent on food. What will you pay him with? If you do not fall into hell or among the hungry ghosts, you are sure to wear horns and fur. How painful, how sad, to leave home like this!

Good people, take advantage of this time before you are old and sick, and make a plan for living [a real Buddhist life] soon. Firmly uphold a vegetarian diet and maintain the precepts, recite the buddha-name and chant the scriptures, pay homage to the buddhas and vow to seek birth in the Pure Land.

After you get to see Amitabha, you will be able to deliver your parents and repay the fourfold benevolence and rescue sentient beings and enjoy eternal happiness. Only if you leave home like this are you a child of Buddha.

## Being a Moral Person

Lung-shu said:

Everyone can be a superior person, a moral person, but they are unwilling to be.

No one needs to be a petty person, a self-seeking person, but they want to be.

To be sincere and faithful and respectful, to be amiable and harmonious and upright, to promote the worthy and praise the good, to benefit beings according to what is appropriate: all such things are the deeds of a superior person, of a moral person. And they are not hard to do. But people are unwilling -- why?

To be devious and tricky and arrogant, to be coarse and violent and deceptive, to speak of shortcomings and exhibit evils, to indulgence whims and injure beings: all such things are the deeds of a petty person, of a self-seeking person. What is the benefit in doing them? But people are determined to do them -- why?

If you are a superior person, people will be pleased with you, the spirits will help you, and misfortune will not occur. You can seek good fortune and riches and you will gain much. ...

If you are a petty person, people will hate you, the spirits will be angry with you, and disasters will come to you. Your good fortune and lifespan will be cut short, and you will suffer many losses. ...

## Perfect Pure Land Practice

Zen Master Yen-shou of Yung-ming said:

The phenomenon of meditative concentration *samadhi* is the basis of the four forms of eloquence and the six supernatural powers. It is the causal basis for reforming ordinary habits and following in the footsteps of the sages. Gathering in mindfulness even for a short time is therefore acclaimed as a great good.

Nevertheless, you must recognize when you are lost in oblivion. The scripture says:

> If you are sitting in meditation and you begin to black out, you must get up and recite the buddha-name while walking, or do ablutions and perform sincere repentance in order to remove the heavy barriers [of bad karma]. Arouse your body and mind. You should not cling to one method and consider it the ultimate.

Some have attained salvation by reciting the buddha-name and chanting scriptures.

Some have been saved by upholding the precepts and preaching the Dharma.

Some have gotten deliverance by earnestly practicing austerities.

Some have been saved by bowing to Buddha and repenting their sins.

Some have attained salvation by seeing the light of Buddha.

Some have been saved by making offerings to the Buddha, Dharma, and Sangha.

Some have been delivered by decorating and sculpting statues of Buddha.

Some have been delivered by painting and drawing images of Buddha.

Some have attained salvation by giving charity and practicing virtue.

Some have been saved by urging people to recite the buddha-name.

Some have attained deliverance by warning against killing living beings and by releasing animals.

Some have been saved by wholeheartedly listening to the Dharma.

Thus we know that if we comprehend the boundless net of the teachings, we return to reality. If we enter the countless gates of salvation, we are all liberated.

It is like making a long journey -- the objective is to arrive at the destination. Do not seize upon the journey and arbitrarily divide it into hard and easy sections. Thus the *Lotus Sutra* says:

> Even if you recite the buddha-name with a scattered mind or praise buddha in a low voice, or scratch out a picture of buddha with your fingernail, or make a stupa out of a pile of sand, and thus gradually accumulate merit, all of you have achieved enlightenment.[44]

So if you understand the One Mind and cultivate the myriad practices, how could you not achieve enlightenment?

## Correct Mindfulness When Facing Death

*Question:*
Master Shan-tao said:

> There is nothing in the world more important than birth and death. Once your breath stops coming, you

are in the next world.  If your mindfulness goes wrong,
then you fall into the cycle of birth and death.

I have often received instructions in the method of
reciting the buddha-name and being born in the Pure
Land, and the principles are very clear.  But I am afraid
that when sickness comes and death approaches, my mind
will be scattered in confusion, and I worry that other
people will disturb my correct mindfulness.  Then I will
forget the basis for the Pure Land.  I humbly hope you
will instruct me again in the method for direct return [to
the Pure Land] and enable me to escape the pain of
sinking down [into the cycle of birth and death].


*Tsung-pen said:*

What an excellent question!  All people who are about
to die want to be born in the Pure Land.  It is necessary
that you not fear death.  Always remember that this body
is fraught with much suffering and impurity.  It is a
painful zone where all kinds of evil karma meet to satisfy
physical desires.  To pass beyond it and be born in the
Pure Land and receive immeasurable happiness and escape
from the painful zone of birth and death is something
that will please you.  It is like taking off filthy clothing
and changing into a bejeweled garment.
    Just abandon body and mind -- do not be attached to
them.
    When you are sick, be mindful of impermanence, and
singlemindedly wait for death.  Instruct your family
members and the people who come to look in on you and

ask about your health and tell them this: "Whoever comes before me must recite the buddha-name for me. Do not talk of the miscellaneous idle matters, or how well or badly various family members are doing. Do not use gentle words to soothe me or express wishes that I be at peace and happy. These are all empty flowers, words that do no good."

If your illness becomes serious and you are facing the end, your relatives should not weep and wail and utter sounds of lamentation and distress. This may throw your mind into confusion and make you lose correct mindfulness. They should just join together and recite the buddha-name to help you go to the Pure Land. Only after your breathing has stopped for a long time can they weep and wail.

As soon as there is the least bit of longing for the world, it immediately becomes an obstruction, and you will not achieve liberation. If you find people who clearly understand the Pure Land, let them come frequently to urge you on and encourage you.[45] This would be a great good fortune.

If you act like this, you are sure to be born in the Pure Land, without a doubt.

*Question*
Should we seek doctors and take medicine or not?

*Answer*
There is nothing wrong with seeking doctors and taking medicine. But medicine can only cure disease, it

cannot save you from fate. If your allotted lifetime is over, medicine can do nothing. But it is not permissible to kill animals to make medicine.[46]

*Question*

What about praying to the spirits?

*Answer*

The length of a person's life is already fixed at birth: how can the spirits prolong it?

If you are deluded by superstition and believe in falsehoods and kill animals in order to sacrifice to the spirits, you are just adding to your evil karma and shortening you life.

If your allotted lifespan is at an end, what can petty spirits do? You are exciting yourself in vain, to no avail.

You should carry out these instructions carefully. Copy out this text and hang it up where you can see it all the time, so you will not forget it when you are facing the end.

*Question*

Can people who have never recited the buddha-name throughout their lives still make use [of these instructions]?

*Answer*

This method can be used by clergy and laypeople, by men and women, and by people who have not recited the buddha-name. All will achieve birth in the Pure Land, without a doubt.

I have seen many people in the world who during
their lives have recited the buddha-name, have paid
homage to buddha, and have made vows to be born in the
Pure Land, but when sickness comes, they are still afraid
of death. They say nothing at all about being born in the
Pure Land or the business of liberation. When their
breathing stops and their lives are about to end and their
consciousness descends into the realms of darkness, then
at last they begin to do ten recitations of the
buddha-name. This is like sounding the alarm after the
robbers have gone out the gate -- what good does it do?

How you act in the gate of death is important. It
takes your own effort to succeed. If your mindfulness
goes astray, you will suffer through the ages: no one will
take your place. Think about it! Think about it!

When [death is imminent] and there is nothing that
can be done, you must make energetic progress in reciting
the buddha-name, and maintain your mindfulness of
buddha with all your strength.

Then for the great matter at the moment of death, we
can say of you: "A single road extends to the West -- you
return directly home, without having to ask the way
there."[47]

# Notes

1. All evil karma results, ultimately, from delusion, the antithesis of enlightenment. Correct practice leads to awakening and enlightenment and thus dissolves away evil karma. It is as though a house were boarded up for ten thousand years. As soon as a window is opened, eons of darkness disappear in a split second.

The dissolution of evil karma through buddha-remembrance can be explained in another way:

A non-individualistic interpretation of the law of karma is provided by the doctrine of *parinamana* or "turning over" of merits. According to this doctrine, the merits which one person has acquired by the performance of good actions, can, if he so wishes, be transferred to another ... By sincerely invoking his name, which is in reality identical with Amitabha himself, we identify ourselves with Amitabha. As a result of this identification, a portion of his merits is transferred to us. These merits, which are now ours, are sufficient not only to counterbalance the effects of our evil actions but also to ensure our rebirth in the Pure Land. The law of karma has not been suspended for our benefit. All that has happened is that a more powerful karma has cancelled out one that was weaker. (Sangharakshita, *A Survey of Buddhism*, p. 375.)

2. This is the essence of the Eighteenth Vow of the future Amitabha Buddha, as described in the *Longer Amitabha Sutra*.

3. See the following passage from the *Amitabha Sutra*:

Shariputra: do not say of these birds that they are in fact the products of evil karma. Why should you not? In that Buddha's land, there is none of the three evil states ... All these various birds are the Amida itself, transformed for the purpose of carrying far and wide the sound of the Dharma. (Hozen Seki, *The Buddha Tells of the Infinite [Amitabha Sutra]*, p.34.)

Another way of understanding this metaphor of birds (or trees) teaching the Dharma, is to recall that self-enlightened Buddhas realized the truth of impermanence "by observing natural phenomena, such as the scattering of blossoms or the falling of leaves."

4. See the following passage:

As an analogy, for a student to exert his own efforts to the utmost is, of course, a laudable thing. If, in addition, he has the benefit of an excellent teacher, who follows his progress and assists him, his level of achievement will be higher, resulting in a sure success in his endeavors. Adding other-power to self-power is similar ... (Thích Thiên Tâm, *Buddhism of Wisdom and Faith*, section 18, question 1.)

5. Please note, however, that buddha-remembrance (Buddha Recitation) as described here has essentially become a Zen method with the goal of reaching awakening. For the koan of Buddha Recitation as a safety net, see Glossary under "Zen."

> If we were to use Buddha Recitation to discover the Mind-Ground and awaken to our Original Nature, the Pure Land method would be no different from other methods. However, when we rely on Buddha Recitation to seek rebirth in the Pure Land, this method has unique characteristics. (Ibid., sect. 27.)

The strength and pervasiveness of Pure Land are such that its main practice, buddha-remembrance (recitation), is found in other schools, including the Tantric and Zen schools. In Pure Land, recitation is practiced for the immediate purpose of achieving rebirth in the Land of Amitabha Buddha. In the Tantric school, the immediate aim is to destroy evil karma and afflictions and generate blessings and wisdom in the current lifetime. In Zen, the koan of buddha-remembrance is meant to sever delusive thought and realize the Self-Nature True Mind. The ultimate goal of all three schools is, of course, the same: to achieve enlightenment and Buddhahood.

A question that immediately arises is how two methods seemingly so opposite as Pure Land and Zen can lead to the same goal of Buddhahood. As an analogy, supposing a patient is admitted to the hospital with a high fever. The physician will, of course, prescribe a medication to lower the fever. However, if later in the day, her temperature has dropped to a dangerously low level, he will attempt to raise it with another prescription. The immediate goal is different in each case, but the ultimate goal in both is the same: to normalize the temperature of the patient. The Buddha, as the master physician, likewise employs 84,000 methods to treat the 84,000 afflictions of sentient beings.

6. This passage refers to a story in which Vimalakirti reassured two monks that they had committed adultery and "murder" involuntarily, without intent. Therefore, since their minds were not polluted, they could repent their transgressions and remain within the Order.

7. See note 1.

8. See Glossary, "Five Precepts."

9. See Glossary, "Third Lifetime."

10. A monk or nun who does not cultivate while receiving offerings from the laity has betrayed the latter's trust and, in effect, stolen the offerings. He has, therefore, incurred immense suffering for the future. The Buddha referred to such monks or nuns as "bald-headed thieves."

11. See Glossary, "Once-Returner."

12. "Horizontal" and "vertical" are figures of speech, which can readily be understood through the following example. Suppose we have a worm, born inside a stalk of bamboo. To escape, it can take the "hard way" and crawl all the way to the top of the stalk. Alternatively, it can look for or poke a hole near its current location and escape "horizontally" into the big, wide world. The horizontal escape, for sentient beings, is to seek rebirth in the Pure Land of Amitabha Buddha.

13. Three factors, faith, vows and practice, are the cornerstones of Pure Land Buddhism. If they are present, rebirth in the Pure Land is assured. *Faith* means faith in Amitabha Buddha's Vows to rescue all who recite His name, as well as faith in one's own Self-Nature, which is intrinsically the same as His (to recite the Buddha's name is to recite the Mind). *Vows* are the determination to be reborn in the Pure Land -- in one's pure mind -- so as to be in the position to save oneself and others. *Practice* generally means reciting the Buddha's name to the point where one's mind and that of Amitabha Buddha are in unison -- i.e., to the point of singlemindedness. Samadhi and wisdom are then achieved.

Please note that all Buddhist teachings are expedients, dividing the one and indivisible Truth into many parts. Faith, vows and practice, although three, are really one. Thus, it can be said that rebirth in the Pure Land depends on three conditions or two conditions (faith and vows) or even one condition (faith), as the one contains all and all are contained in the one. The formula to be used depends on the audience and the times. The aim is to enable sentient beings to achieve rebirth in the Pure Land as a steppingstone toward Buddhahood.

14. According to Buddhist teaching, keeping the five precepts results in rebirth in human form, while keeping the ten precepts results in rebirth as a deva (deity). Since the human and celestial realms are still subject to birth and death, however, rebirth there is not the goal of Pure Land Buddhists. They seek rebirth in the Land of Amitabha Buddha, a realm transcending birth and death.

15. See also *Buddhism of Wisdom and Faith*, sect. 30.4.

16. See note 1.

17. See note 13.

18. According to Buddhist teachings, if there were another obstruction as strong as love-attachment, no cultivator could ever hope to attain Buddhahood.

19. To be truly effective in dedicating merit to others, the practitioner must be utterly sincere and singleminded in his recitation. Even so, the sutras teach that the recipient can only obtain a small part of this merit. Furthermore, since the crucial conditions of sincerity and singlemindedness are seldom achieved in full, most intercessions are, at best, partially effective and can seldom erase a lifetime of bad karma. Thus, it is imperative for the practitioner himself to cultivate, and not rely entirely on monks and nuns.

20. See Glossary, "Zen" for an explanation of the Great Doubt (True Doubt).

21. See note 13.

22. Recent commentaries have suggested that this reference, taken from the sutras, anticipates the advent of the Atomic Age by some 25 centuries. The splitting of the atom (smallest blade of grass) can release immense power, which, at the end of the Dharma-Ending Age, is unimaginably destructive.

23. A translation of Master Chih-i's commentary *Ten Doubts about Pure Land* appears in Thích Thiên Tâm, tr., *Pure Land Buddhism: Dialogues with Ancient Masters.*

24. In Buddhism, the number seven has a mystical significance. Thus, the traditional mourning period is forty-nine (seven times seven) days. See also *Buddhism of Wisdom and Faith*, sect. 44.

25. This section refers to the first meditation in the *Meditation Sutra*, in which Queen Vaidehi was taught to "gaze upon the sun, hanging like a suspended drum, when it is about to set."

26. This reference is explained in the following koan:

> The wind was making the temple flag flutter. There were two monks arguing. One said the flag was moving. One said the wind was moving. They argued back and forth without reaching the truth.
> The Sixth Patriarch said to them, "It is not the wind moving, and it is not the flag moving. It is your minds that are moving."
> The two monks were startled. (J.C. Cleary, *Meditating with Koans*, p. 124.)

27. In Buddhism, regardless of the school, *practice* (cultivation) is a must. A Buddhist who merely studies or lectures on the Buddha's teaching while failing to put it into practice has been likened to a sick doctor who prescribes medicines for others while refusing to take any himself.

According to Buddhist teachings, we all have within us varying degrees of greed, anger and delusion. To practice is to avoid or mitigate the *conditions* that promote greed, anger and delusion. Thus, for example, whenever anger flares up, one's thoughts should be redirected, as a form of displacement, toward the Buddha through buddha-remembrance (Buddha Recitation).

28. This is a well-known image from the *Avatamsaka Sutra*:

> It is as [if] there is a great scripture/Equal in extent to
> a universe/Existing inside one atom,/And in all atoms

as well;/Someone with intelligence and wisdom/Sees all clearly with pure eyes/And breaks the atoms, releasing the scriptures/for the benefit of all beings./Buddha-knowledge, likewise,/Is in all beings' minds ... (Thomas Cleary, tr. *The Flower Ornament Sutra*, Vol. II, p. 317.)

29. Please note the high-level nature of Master Tsung-pen's inquiry. It is to escape birth and death that he seeks the Dharma and not for wealth or good health or other such mundane aspirations.

30. See note 1.

31. Killing sentient beings, including slaughtering animals for food, is among the heaviest transgressions in Buddhism. This is not only because such acts create untold suffering and contradict the spirit of compassion, but also because they cut short the lives of future Buddhas (as all sentient beings have a common Buddha Nature).

32. By de-emphasizing the role of teachers and gurus, thus freeing practitioners from mediating authority figures, the Pure Land school effectively empowers practitioners.

33. To see "reality nature," i.e., one's true mind, is the immediate goal of Zen meditation.

34. This concept from the *Avatamsaka Sutra* can be understood through the analogy of apple seeds (causes) leading to the apples of the future (results); the apples (results), in turn, contain within themselves the seeds (causes) of future trees and apples. In the same vein, sentient beings (causes) have the Buddha Nature within themselves, leading to Buddhahood (results) in the future; these Buddhas (results), in time, return

to the world to rescue sentient beings (causes). Thus, cause and result are inseparable -- cause is result, result is cause.

35. Translations of Master Chih-i's commentary "Ten Doubts about Pure Land" and Master T'ien-ju's treatise "Questions about the Pure Land" appear in Thích Thiên Tâm, *Pure Land Buddhism: Dialogues with Ancient Masters*. See Bibliography for details.

36. There are many sets of precepts (discipline) in Buddhism, for laypeople, novices, monks and nuns, etc. However, they all derive from the three fundamental precepts of the Bodhisattva: "do not commit any of the forms of evil; faithfully practice the many virtues; universally deliver sentient beings." In a similar vein, the *Dhammapada Sutra*, a key text of the Theravada School, states: "Do not what is evil. Do what is good. Keep your mind pure." Note that the last injunction differs, reflecting the different emphases of the Mahayana and Theravada schools.

37. For example, the Patriarch Dogen, the founder of the Japanese Soto Zen school, held that only monks and nuns could achieve true enlightenment through Zen. For details, see Kenneth Kraft, *Zen: Tradition and Transition*, p. 186.

38. Dead Tree Samadhi. After a cultivator has reached a fairly high level of samadhi, he experiences ethereal bliss. However, he must progress beyond that level to develop wisdom. Otherwise, he is said to be mired in "dead tree" samadhi, a form of attachment which will effectively prevent him from reaching the Way. A famous koan illustrates this point:

> Once there was a devoted old woman who built a place
> of retreat for a monk, arranging that he would not lack

for anything, so that he could concentrate upon his meditation and practice. One day, after twenty years, she instructed her daughter: "Today, after serving the Master his meal, take advantage of the situation to embrace him tightly, asking him at the same time, 'how does it feel to be hugged these days?' Come back and let me know his answer as faithfully as you can."

The daughter dutifully did as she was told, putting her arms around the Master and asking the question. The Master replied, "I am not moved in the very least by sexual desire, no different from a *dried up tree* leaning against a cold mass of rocks in the middle of winter, when not even a drop of warmth can be found." The young girl repeated the answer to her mother, who said unhappily, "I have really wasted my time and effort during the last twenty years. Little did I know that I was only supporting a common mortal!" Having said this, she went out, evicted the monk, lit a fire and burned the meditation hut to the ground.

39.    All these scenes viewed by the cultivator while in meditation are referred to as demons. This is so because they disturb the mind.

40. In Buddhism, the higher levels of truth cannot be grasped through mere intellectual understanding or reasoning. In fact, all reasoning, based on our limited senses and faculties, is a hindrance. The Buddhist analogy is that of a person attempting to lift a chair while seated upon it!

41. Non-retrogression to the realm of birth and death is a key advantage of rebirth in the Pure Land (compared, for example, to rebirth in the Tushita Heaven, etc).

42. In Buddhism, the body is often referred to as a "stinking bag of skin," with nine orifices from which ooze out all manner of foul-smelling fluids. This image is meant to break attachment to the body, the main affliction of sentient beings.

43. This is a reference to the story of an exceptional parrot contained in the *Biographies of Pure Land Sages and Saints*, a famous collection of rebirth stories not available in English.

44. This passage expresses a crucial Mahayana teaching. We all have the buddha nature within us, but it is hidden by delusion. If, through a good action (reciting the buddha-name, drawing an image of the Buddha in the sand, etc.) a cultivator has calmed the turbid waters of his mind, he has, in effect, recovered his Buddhahood -- he has achieved Buddhahood *for that moment.*

> Even if little boys in play/ should use a piece of grass or wood or a brush,/ or perhaps a fingernail/ to draw an image of the Buddha,/such persons as these .../all have attained the Buddha Way. (Burton Watson, tr. *The Lotus Sutra*, p. 39.)

This, of course, does not mean that he has the same spiritual powers as the Buddha, but that his mind is now the mind of a Buddha -- and that is the first step. If he can achieve this, then although he may dwell in the realm of birth and death, he no longer fears birth and death; birth and death can no longer pollute his mind.

45. For details on the last rites and on the duties of a Good Spiritual Advisor, please refer to *Buddhism of Wisdom and Faith*, Chap. X, particularly, section 69. The essential point is

to help the dying person keep his mind empty and still by focussing on the Buddha's name.

46. See note 31.

47. The West (the Pure Land) is the cultivator's home. To be reborn in the Pure land is to return home, to return to one's mind. This is the essence of Mind-Only Pure Land, the essence of Zen.

# *Glossary*

**Amitabha (Amida, Amita, Amitayus).** Amitabha is the most commonly used name for the Buddha of Infinite Light and Infinite Life. A transhistorical Buddha venerated by all Mahayana schools (T'ien T'ai, Esoteric, Zen ...) and, particularly, Pure Land. Presides over the Western Pure Land (Land of Ultimate Bliss), where anyone can be reborn through utterly sincere recitation of His name, particularly at the time of death.

Amitabha Buddha at the highest or noumenon level represents the True Mind, the Self-Nature common to the Buddhas and sentient beings – all-encompassing and all-inclusive. This deeper understanding provides the rationale for the harmonization of Zen and Pure Land, two of the most popular schools of Mahayana Buddhism. See also "Buddha Recitation," "Mind," Pure Land."

**Amitabha Sutra.** See "Three Pure land Sutras."

**Arhat.** Arhatship is the highest rank attained by Sravakas. An Arhat is a Buddhist saint who has attained liberation from the cycle of Birth and Death, generally through living a monastic life in accordance with the Buddhas' teachings. This is the goal of Theravadin practice, as contrasted with Bodhisattvahood in Mahayana practice. (*A Dictionary of Buddhism.*)  See also "Sravakas."

**Attachment.** In the Four Noble truths, Buddha Shakyamuni taught that attachment to self is the root cause of suffering:

> From craving [attachment] springs grief, from craving springs fear; For him who is wholly free from craving, there is no grief, much less fear. (*Dhammapada Sutra.* In Narada Maha Thera, *The Buddha and His Teachings.*)

> If you don't have attachments, naturally you're liberated ... In ancient times, there was an old cultivator who asked for instructions from a monk, "Great Monk, let me ask you, how can I attain liberation?"  The Great monk said, "Who tied you up?"  This old cultivator answered, "Nobody tied me up."  The monk said, "Then why do you seek liberation?" (Hsuan Hua, tr., *Flower Adornment Sutra*, "Pure Conduct," chap. 11.)

For the seasoned practitioner, even the Dharma must not become an attachment.  As an analogy, to clean one's shirt, it is necessary to use soap.  However, if the soap is not then rinsed out, the garment will not be truly clean.  Similarly, the practitioner's mind will not be fully liberated until he severs attachment to everything, including the Dharma itself.

**Avalokitesvara.** Also called Kuan Yin, the Bodhisattva of Compassion. Usually recognizable by the small Buddha adorning Her crown.

**Avatamsaka (Flower Ornament) Sutra.** The basic text of the Avatamsaka School. It is one of the longest sutras in the Buddhist Canon and records the highest teaching of Buddha Shakyamuni, immediately after Enlightenment. It is traditionally believed that the Sutra was taught to the Bodhisattvas and other high spiritual beings while the Buddha was in samadhi. The Sutra has been described as the "epitome of Buddhist thought, Buddhist sentiment and Buddhist experience" and is quoted by all schools of Mahayana Buddhism, in particular, Pure Land and Zen.

**Awakening vs. Enlightenment.** A clear distinction should be made between *awakening to the Way* (Great Awakening) and *attaining the Way* (attaining Enlightenment). (Note: There are many degrees of Awakening and Enlightenment. Attaining the Enlightenment of the Arhats, Pratyeka Buddhas, Bodhisattvas, etc. is different from attaining *Supreme Enlightenment*, i.e., Buddhahood.)

To experience a Great Awakening is to achieve (through Zen meditation, Buddha Recitation, etc.) a complete and deep realization of what it means to be a Buddha and how to reach Buddhahood. It is to see one's Nature, comprehend the True Nature of things, the Truth. However, only after becoming a Buddha can one be said to have truly attained Supreme Enlightenment (attained the Way). A metaphor appearing in the sutras is that of a glass of water containing sediments. As long as the glass is undisturbed, the sediments remain at the bottom and the water is clear. However, as soon as the glass is shaken, the water becomes turbid. Likewise, when a

practitioner experiences a Great Awakening (awakens to the
Way), his afflictions (greed, anger and delusion) are temporarily
suppressed but not yet eliminated. To achieve Supreme
Enlightenment (i.e., to be rid of all afflictions, to discard all
sediments) is the ultimate goal. Only then can he completely
trust his mind and actions. Before then, he should adhere to
the precepts, keep a close watch on his mind and thoughts, like
a cat stalking a mouse, ready to pounce on evil thoughts as
soon as they arise. To do otherwise is to court certain failure,
as stories upon stories of errant monks, roshis and gurus
demonstrate.

**Awakening of the Faith (Treatise).** A major commentary by
the Patriarch Asvaghosha (1st/2nd cent.), which presents the
fundamental principles of Mahayana Buddhism. Several
translations exist in English.

**Bodhi.** Sanskrit for Enlightenment.

**Bodhi Mind, (Bodhicitta, Great Mind).** The spirit of
Enlightenment, the aspiration to achieve it, the Mind set on
Enlightenment. It involves two parallel aspects: i) the
determination to achieve Buddhahood and ii) the aspiration to
rescue all sentient beings.

**Bodhisattvas.** Those who aspire to Supreme Enlightenment
and Buddhahood for themselves and all beings. The word
Bodhisattva can therefore stand for a realized being such as
Avalokitesvara or Samantabhadra but also for anyone who has
developed the Bodhi Mind, the aspiration to save oneself and
others.

**Brahma Net Sutra (Brahmajala Sutra).** This is a sutra of
major significance in Mahayana Buddhism. In addition to

containing the ten major precepts of Mahayana (not to kill, steal, lie, etc.) the Sutra also contains forty-eight less important injunctions. These fifty-eight major and minor precepts constitute the Bodhisattva Precepts, taken by most Mahayana monks and nuns and certain advanced lay practitioners.

**Buddha Nature.** The following terms refer to the same thing: Self-Nature, True Nature, Original Nature, Dharma Nature, True Mark, True Mind, True Emptiness, True Thusness, Dharma Body, Original Face, Emptiness, Prajna, Nirvana, etc.

> According to the Mahayana view, [buddha-nature] is the true, immutable, and eternal nature of all beings. Since all beings possess buddha-nature, it is possible for them to attain enlightenment and become a buddha, regardless of what level of existence they occupy ... The answer to the question whether buddha-nature is immanent in beings is an essential determining factor for the association of a given school with Theravada or Mahayana, the two great currents within Buddhism. In Theravada this notion is unknown; here the potential to become a buddha is not ascribed to every being. By contrast the Mahayana sees the attainment of buddhahood as the highest goal; it can be attained through the inherent buddha-nature of every being through appropriate spiritual practice. (*The Shambhala Dictionary of Buddhism and Zen.*)

See also "Dharma Nature."

**Buddha Recitation (Buddha-Remembrance).** General term for a number of practices, such as i) oral recitation of Amitabha Buddha's name and ii) visualization/contemplation of His auspicious marks and those of the Pure Land.

In reciting the buddha-name you use your own mind to be mindful of your own true self: how could this be considered seeking outside yourself? (Cited in J.C. Cleary, *Meditating with koans*.)

Reciting the buddha-name proceeds from the mind. The mind remembers Buddha and does not forget. That's why it is called buddha remembrance, or reciting the buddha-name mindfully. (This book, p. 92.)

The most common Pure Land technique is recitation of Amitabha Buddha's name. See also "Amitabha," "Pure Land."

**Dedication of Merit.** See "Transference of Merit."

**Degenerate Age.** See "Dharma-Ending Age."

**Delusion (Ignorance).** "Delusion refers to belief in something that contradicts reality. In Buddhism, delusion is ... a lack of awareness of the true nature or Buddha nature of things, or of the true meaning of existence. "According to the Buddhist outlook, we are deluded by our senses -- among which intellect (discriminating, discursive thought) is included as a sixth sense. Consciousness, attached to the senses, leads us into error by causing us to take the world of appearances for the world of reality, whereas in fact it is only a limited and fleeting aspect of reality." (*Shambhala Dictionary of Buddhism and Zen*.)

**Demons.** Evil influences which hinder cultivation. These can take an infinite number of forms, including evil beings or hallucinations. Disease and death, as well as the three poisons of greed, anger and delusion are also equated to demons, as they disturb the mind.

The *Nirvana Sutra* lists four types of demon: i) greed, anger and delusion; ii) the five skandas, or obstructions caused by physical and mental functions; iii) death; iv) the demon of the Sixth Heaven (Realm of Desire).

The Self-Nature has been described in Mahayana sutras as a house full of gold and jewelry. To preserve the riches, i.e., to keep the mind calm, empty and still, we should shut the doors to the three thieves of greed, anger and delusion. Letting the mind wander opens the house to "demons," that is, hallucinations and harm. Thus, Zen practitioners are taught that, while in meditation, "Encountering demons, kill the demons, encountering Buddhas, kill the Buddhas." Both demons and Buddhas are mind-made, Mind-Only.

For a detailed discussion of demons, see Master Thích Thiền Tâm, *Buddhism of Wisdom and Faith*, sect. 51.

**Devas.** Deities, gods.

**Dharma.**    a) The teachings of the Buddhas (generally capitalized in English); b) duty, law, doctrine; c) things, events, phenomena, everything.

**Dharma-Ending Age, Degenerate Age, Last Age.**    The present spiritually degenerate era, twenty-six centuries after the demise of Shakyamuni Buddha.    The concept of decline, dissension and schism within the Dharma after the passing of the Buddha is a general teaching of Buddhism and a corollary to the Truth of Impermanence. See, for example, the *Diamond Sutra* (sect. 6 in the translation by A.F. Price and Wong Mou-lam).    The time following Buddha Shakyamuni's demise is divided into three periods: i) the Perfect Age of the Dharma, lasting 500 years, when the Buddha's teaching (usually meditation) was correctly practiced and Enlightenment often attained; ii) the Dharma Semblance Age, lasting about 1,000 years, when a form of the teaching was practiced but Enlightenment seldom attained; iii) the Dharma-Ending Age, lasting some ten thousand years, when a diluted form of the teaching exists and Enlightenment is rarely attained.

**Dharma Gate.** School, method, tradition.

**Dharma Nature.** The intrinsic nature of all things. Used interchangeably with "emptiness," "reality." See also "Buddha Nature."

**Dharmakara.** The Bodhisattva who later became Amitabha Buddha, as related in the *Longer Amitabha Sutra*. The Bodhisattva Dharmakara is famous for forty-eight Vows, particularly the eighteenth, which promises rebirth in the Pure Land to anyone who recites His name with utmost sincerity and faith at the time of death.

**Diamond Sutra.** "An independent part of the *Prajnaparamita Sutra*, which attained great importance, particularly in East Asia. It shows that all phenomenal appearances are not ultimate reality but rather illusions, projections of one's own mind ... The work is called *Diamond Sutra* because it is 'sharp like a diamond that cuts away all unnecessary conceptualizations and brings one to the further shore of enlightenment.'" (*Shambhala Dictionary of Buddhism and Zen.*)

**Difficult Path of Practice (Path of the Sages, Self-Power Path).** According to Pure Land teaching, all conventional Buddhist ways of practice and cultivation (Zen, Theravada, the Vinaya School ...), which emphasize self-power and self-reliance.

This is contrasted to the Easy Path of Practice, that is, the Pure Land method, which relies on both self-power and other-power (the power and assistance of the Buddhas and Bodhisattvas).

**Dusts (Worldly Dusts).** A metaphor for all the mundane things that can cloud our bright Self-Nature. These include form, sound, scent, taste, touch, dharmas (external opinions and views). These dusts correspond to the five senses and the discriminating, everyday mind (the sixth sense, in Buddhism).

**Easy Path of Practice.** Refers to Pure Land practice. The Easy Path involves reliance on the power of the Buddhas and Bodhisattvas, in particular Buddha Amitabha ("other-power") in addition to one's own cultivation("self-power"). Usually contrasted with primary reliance on self-power (Difficult Path of Practice), taught in other Buddhist schools. Equal reliance on self-power and other-power distinguishes the Pure Land School from most other schools of Buddhism. The distinction is, however, a matter of emphasis, as all schools of Buddhism rely, to a greater or lesser extent, on both self-power and other-power.

**Endurance (World).** See "Saha World."

**Enlightenment.** See "Awakening vs. Enlightenment."

**Evil Paths.** The paths of hells, hungry ghosts, animality. These paths can be taken as states of mind; i.e., when someone has a vicious thought of maiming or killing another, he is effectively reborn, *for that moment*, in the hells.

**Expedient means (Skillful means, Skill-in-means, Upaya).** Refers to strategies, methods, devices, targetted to the capacities, circumstances, likes and dislikes of each sentient being, so as to rescue him and lead him to Enlightenment.    "Thus, all particular formulations of the Teaching are just provisional expedients to communicate the Truth (Dharma) in specific contexts." (J.C. Cleary.) "The Buddha's words were medicines for a given sickness at a given time," always infinitely adaptable to the conditions of the audience.

**Externalists.** Literally, followers of non-Buddhist paths. This term is generally used by Buddhists with reference to followers of other religions.

**Five Desires (Five Sensual Pleasures).** Desires connected with the five senses, i.e., form, sound, aroma, taste and touch.

**Five Precepts.**    The precepts taken by lay Buddhists, prohibiting i) killing, ii) stealing iii) lying, iv) sexual misconduct, v) ingesting intoxicants.  See also "Ten Precepts."

**Flower Store World.** The entire cosmos, consisting of worlds upon worlds *ad infinitum*, as described in the *Avatamsaka Sutra*. It is the realm of Vairocana Buddha, the transcendental aspect of Buddha Shakyamuni and of all Buddhas. The Saha World, the Western Pure Land and, for that matter, all lands and realms are within the Flower Store World.

**Good Spiritual Advisor.** Guru, virtuous friend, wise person, Bodhisattva, Buddha -- anyone (even an evil being!) who can help the practitioner progress along the path to Enlightenment. This notwithstanding, *wisdom* should be the primary factor in the selection of such an advisor: the advisor must have wisdom, and both advisor and practitioner must exercise wisdom in selecting one another.

**Great Awakening.** See "Awakening vs. Enlightenment."

**Heretical views.** The sutras usually refer to sixty-two such views. They are the externalist (non-Buddhist) views prevalent in Buddha Shakyamuni's time.

**Karma.** Action leading to future retribution or reward, in the current or future lifetimes.

Common karma: the difference between personal and common karma can be seen in the following example: Suppose a country goes to war to gain certain economic advantages and in the process, numerous soldiers and civilians are killed or maimed. If a particular citizen volunteers for military service and actually participates in the carnage, he commits a *personal* karma of killing. Other citizens, however, even if opposed to the war, may benefit directly or indirectly (e.g., through economic gain). They are thus said to share in the *common* karma of killing of their country.

Fixed karma: in principle, all karma is subject to change. Fixed karma, however, is karma which can only be changed in extraordinary circumstances, because it derives from an evil act committed simultaneously with mind, speech and body. An example of fixed karma would be a premeditated crime (versus a crime of passion).

**Lankavatara Sutra.** The only sutra recommended by Bodhidharma, the First Zen Patriarch in China. It is a key Zen text, along with the *Diamond Sutra* (recommended by the Sixth Patriarch), the *Surangama Sutra*, the *Vimalakirti Sutra*, the *Avatamsaka Sutra* ... The last four sutras are referred to frequently in Pure Land commentaries.

**Last Age.** See "Dharma-Ending Age."

**Lotus Grades.** The nine possible degrees of rebirth in the Western Pure Land. The more merits and virtues the practitioner accumulates, the higher the grade.

**Lotus Sutra.** A major Buddhist text and one of the most widely read sutras in the present day.

> One of the earliest and most richly descriptive of the Mahayana sutras of Indian origin. It became important for the shaping of the Buddhist tradition in East Asia, in particular because of its teaching of the One Vehicle under which are subsumed the usual Hinayana [Theravada] and Mahayana divisions. It is the main text of the Tendai [T'ien T'ai] school. (Joji Okazaki.)

This School has a historically close relationship with the Pure Land School. Thus, Master T'ai Hsu taught that the *Lotus Sutra* and the *Amitabha Sutras* were closely connected, differing only in length.

**Lotus Treasury World.** See "Ocean-Wide Lotus Assembly."

**Mahasthamaprapta (Shih Chih, Seishi).** One of the three sages in Pure Land Buddhism, recognizable by the water jar (jewelled pitcher) adorning Her crown. Usually represented in female form in East Asian iconography. Amitabha Buddha is frequently depicted standing between the Bodhisattvas Avalokitesvara and Mahasthamaprapta.

**Marks.** Characteristics, forms, physiognomy. Marks are contrasted with essence, in the same way that phenomena are contrasted with noumenon. *True Mark* stands for True Form, True Nature, Buddha Nature, always unchanging. The *True Mark* of all phenomena is like space: always existing but really empty; although empty, really existing. The *True Mark* of the Triple World is No-Birth/No-Death, not existent/not non-existent, not like this/not like that. *True Mark* is also called "Self-Nature," "Dharma Body," the "Unconditioned," "True Thusness," "Nirvana," "Dharma Realm." See also "Noumenon/Phenomena."

**Meditation Sutra.** One of the three core sutras of the Pure Land school. It teaches sixteen methods of visualizing Amitabha Buddha, the Bodhisattvas and the Pure Land. This sutra stresses the element of meditation in Pure Land. See also "Three Pure Land Sutras," "Vaidehi," "Visualization."

**Merit and Virtue.** these two terms are sometimes used interchangeably. However, there is a crucial difference: merits are the blessings (wealth, intelligence, etc.) of the human and celestial realms; therefore, they are temporary and subject to Birth and Death. Virtues, on the other hand, transcend Birth and Death and lead to Buddhahood. Four virtues are mentioned in Pure Land Buddhism: eternity; happiness; True Self; purity.      An identical action (e.g., charity) can lead either to merit or virtue, depending on the mind of the practitioner, that is, on whether he is seeking mundane rewards (merit) or transcendence (virtue). Thus, the Pure Land cultivator should not seek merits for by doing so, he would, in effect, be choosing to remain within samsara. This would be counter to his very wish to escape Birth and Death.

**Mind.** Key concept in all Buddhist teaching.

> Frequent term in Zen, used in two senses: (1) the mind-ground, the One Mind ... the buddha-mind, the mind of thusness ... (2) false mind, the ordinary mind dominated by conditioning, desire, aversion, ignorance,

and false sense of self, the mind of delusion ... (J.C. Cleary, *A Buddha from Korea*.)

The ordinary, deluded mind (thought) includes feelings, impressions, conceptions, consciousness, etc. The Self-Nature True Mind is the fundamental nature, the Original Face, reality, etc. As an analogy, the Self-Nature True Mind is to mind what water is to waves -- the two cannot be dissociated. They are the same but they are also different.          To approach the sutras "making discriminations and nurturing attachments" is no different from the Zen allegory of a person attempting to lift a chair while seated on it. If he would only get off the chair, he could raise it easily.    Similarly, the practitioner truly understands the Dharma only to the extent that he "suspends the operation of the discriminating intellect, the faculty of the internal dialogue through which people from moment to moment define and perpetuate their customary world of perception." (See this book, Introduction.)

See also the following passage:

The mind ... "creates" the world in the sense that it invests the phenomenal world with value. The remedy to this situation, according to Buddhism, is to still the mind, to stop it from making discriminations and nurturing attachments toward certain phenomena and feelings of aversion toward others. When this state of calmness of mind is achieved, the darkness of ignorance and passion will be dispelled and the mind can perceive the underlying unity of the absolute. The individual will then have achieved the state of enlightenment and will be freed from the cycle of birth and death, because such a person is now totally indifferent to them both. (Burton Watson, *The Zen Teachings of Master Lin-Chi*.)

**Mindfulness of the Buddha.** Synonymous with Buddha Recitation. See "Buddha Recitation."

**Nagarjuna.** (2nd/3rd cent.) "One of the most important philosophers of Buddhism and the founder of the Madhyamika school. Nagarjuna's major accomplishment was his systematization ... of the teaching presented in the *Prajnaparamita Sutras.* Nagarjuna's methodological approach of rejecting all opposites is the basis of the Middle Way ..." (*Shambhala Dictionary of Buddhism and Zen.*)

**Non-Birth (No-Birth).** "A term used to describe the nature of Nirvana. In Mahayana Buddhism generally, No-Birth signifies the 'extinction' of the discursive thinking by which we conceive of things as arising and perishing, forming attachments to them." (Ryukoku University.) See also "Tolerance of Non-Birth."

**Ocean-Wide Lotus Assembly.** The Lotus Assembly represents the gathering of Buddha Amitabha, the Bodhisattvas, the sages and saints and all other superior beings in the Land of Ultimate Bliss. This Assembly is "Ocean-Wide" as the participants are infinite in number -- spreading as far and wide as the ocean. The term Ocean-Wide Assembly is generally associated with the *Avatamsaka Sutra*, a text particularly prized by the Pure Land and Zen schools alike.

**Once-returner.** A sage who has only one rebirth left before reaching Arhatship and escaping birth and death.

**One-Life Bodhisattva.** A Bodhisattva who is one lifetime away from Buddhahood. The best known example is the Bodhisattva Maitreya.

**Other-Power.** See "Easy Path of Practice."

**Polar Mountain.** In Buddhist cosmology, the universe is composed of worlds upon worlds, ad infinitum. (Our earth is only a small part of one of these worlds). The Polar Mountain is the central mountain of each world.

**Pratyeka Buddhas.** "These buddhas become fully enlightened ... by meditating on the principle of causality. Unlike the Perfect Buddhas, however, they do not exert themselves to teach others" (A. Buzo and T. Prince).

**Pure Land.** Generic term for the realms of the Buddhas. In this text it denotes the Land of Ultimate Bliss or Western Land of Amitabha Buddha. It is not a realm of enjoyment, but rather an *ideal place of cultivation*, beyond the Triple Realm and samsara, where those who are reborn are no longer subject to retrogression. This is the key distinction between the Western Pure Land and such realms as the Tusita Heaven. There are two conceptions of the Pure Land: as different and apart from the Saha World *and* as one with and the same as the Saha World. When the mind is pure and undefiled, any land or environment becomes a pure land (*Vimalakirti, Avatamsaka Sutras* ...). See also "Triple Realm."

**Pure Land School.** When Mahayana Buddhism spread to China, Pure Land ideas found fertile ground for development. In the fourth century, the movement crystallized with the formation of the Lotus Society, founded by Master Hui Yuan (334-416), the first Pure Land Patriarch. The school was formalized under the Patriarchs T'an Luan (Donran) and Shan Tao (Zendo). Master Shan Tao's teachings, in particular, greatly influenced the development of Japanese Pure Land, associated with Honen Shonin (Jodo school) and his disciple,

Shinran Shonin (Jodo Shinshu school) in the 12th and 13th centuries. Jodo Shinshu, or Shin Buddhism, places overwhelming emphasis on the element of faith.

> [Pure Land comprises the schools] of East Asia which emphasize aspects of Mahayana Buddhism stressing faith in Amida, meditation on and recitation of his name, and the religious goal of being reborn in his "Pure Land" or "Western Paradise." (Keith Crim.)

Note: An early form of Buddha Recitation can be found in the *Nikayas* of the Pali Canon:

> In the *Nikayas*, the Buddha ... advised his disciples to think of him and his virtues as if they saw his body before their eyes, whereby they would be enabled to accumulate merit and attain Nirvana or be saved from transmigrating in the evil paths ... (D.T. Suzuki, *The Eastern Buddhist*, Vol. 3, No. 4, p. 317.)

**Pure Land Sutras.** See "Three Pure Land Sutras."

**Saha World.** World of Endurance. Refers to this world of ours, filled with suffering and afflictions, yet gladly endured by its inhabitants.

**Samadhi.** Meditative absorption. "Usually denotes the particular final stage of pure concentration." There are many degrees and types of samadhi (Buddha Recitation, Ocean Seal, Pratyutpanna ...)

**Samantabhadra.** Also called Universal Worthy or, in Japanese, Fugen. A major Bodhisattva, who personifies the transcendental practices and vows of the Buddhas (as compared to the Bodhisattva Manjusri, who represents transcendental wisdom). Usually depicted seated on an elephant with six tusks (six paramitas). Best known for his "Ten Great Vows."

**Samatha-Vipasyana.** "Tranquility and contemplation; stopping evil thoughts and meditating on the truth." (Hisao Inagaki.)

**Samsara.** Cycle of rebirths; realms of Birth and Death.

**Sariputra.** Major disciple of Shakyamuni Buddha, foremost in wisdom among His Arhat disciples.

**Self-Power.** See "Difficult Path of Practice."

**Seven Treasures.** Gold, silver, lapis lazuli, crystal, agate, red pearl and carnelian. They represent the seven powers of faith, perseverance, sense of shame, avoidance of wrongdoing, mindfulness, concentration and wisdom.

**Six Directions.** North, South, East, West, above and below, i.e., all directions. In the *Avatamsaka Sutra*, they are expanded to include points of the compass in between and are referred to as the Ten Directions.

**Six Dusts.** See "Dusts."

**Six Planes of Existence (Six Paths).** The paths within the realm of Birth and Death. Includes the three Evil Paths (hells, hungry ghosts, animality) and the paths of humans, asuras and celestials. These paths can be understood as states of mind. See also "Evil Paths."

**Sixth Patriarch.** Hui Neng (638-713), the Sixth Patriarch of the Chinese Zen school and author of the *Platform Sutra*.

**Skillful Means.** See "Expedient Means."

**Spiritual power.** Also called miraculous power. Includes, *inter alia*, the ability to see all forms (deva eye), to hear all sounds (deva ear), to know the thoughts of others, to be anywhere and do anything at will.

**Sravakas.** "Lit., 'voice-hearers': those who follow [Theravada] and eventually become arhats as a result of listening to the buddhas and following their teachings" (A. Buzo and T. Prince.) See also "Arhat."

**Sudhana (Good Wealth).** The main protagonist in the next-to-last and longest chapter of the *Avatamsaka Sutra*. Seeking Enlightenment, he visited and studied with fifty-three spiritual advisors and became the equal of the Buddhas in one lifetime. Both his first advisor and his last advisor (Samantabhadra) taught him the Pure Land path.

**Surangama Sutra.** Also called *Heroic Gate Sutra*.

> The "Sutra of the Heroic One" exercised a great influence on the development of Mahayana Buddhism in China [and neighboring countries]. It emphasizes the power of samadhi, through which enlightenment can be attained, and explains the various methods of emptiness meditation through the practice of which everyone ... can realize ... enlightenment ... (*Shambhala Dictionary of Buddhism and Zen.*)

**Tathagata.** Usually translated as "Thus Come One."

> He who came as did all Buddhas, who took the absolute way of cause and effect, and attained to perfect

wisdom; one of the highest titles of a Buddha (Charles Luk).

**Ten Directions.** See "Six Directions."

**Ten Evil Acts (Ten Evil Deeds, Ten Sins).** 1. Killing; 2. stealing; 3. sexual misconduct; 4. lying; 5. slander; 6. coarse language; 7. empty chatter; 8. covetousness; 9. angry speech; 10. wrong views. (Note: taking intoxicants is not included in this formulation.) See also "Ten Precepts."

**Ten Great Vows.** The famous vows of the Bodhisattva Samantabhadra in the *Avatamsaka Sutra*. These vows represent the quintessence of this Sutra and are the basis of all Mahayana practice. Studying the vows and putting them into practice is tantamount to studying the *Avatamsaka Sutra* and practicing its teachings. See also "Samantabhadra."

**Ten Precepts (Ten Virtues, Ten Good Deeds).** Include an expanded version of the Five Precepts of body and mouth (not to kill, steal, engage in illicit sex, lie, or take intoxicants) with the addition of the virtues of the mind (elimination of greed, anger and delusion). See also "Five Precepts," "Ten Evil Acts."

**Third Lifetime.** In the first lifetime, the practitioner engages in mundane good deeds which bring ephemeral worldly blessings (wealth, power, authority, etc.) in the second lifetime. Since power tends to corrupt, he is likely to create evil karma, resulting in retribution in the third lifetime. Thus, good deeds in the first lifetime are potential "enemies" of the third lifetime.

To ensure that mundane good deeds do not become "enemies," the practitioner should dedicate all merits to a transcendental goal, i.e., to become Bodhisattvas or Buddhas or, in Pure Land teaching, to achieve rebirth in the Pure Land -- a

Buddha land beyond Birth and Death.

In a mundane context, these three lifetimes can be conceived of as three generations. Thus, the patriarch of a prominent family, through hard work and luck, amasses great power, fortune and influence (first lifetime). His children are then able to enjoy a leisurely, and, too often, dissipated life (second lifetime). By the generation of the grandchildren, the family's fortune and good reputation have all but disappeared (third lifetime).

**Three Evil Paths.** See "Evil Paths."

**Three Pure Land Sutras.** Pure Land Buddhism is based on three basic sutras:

a) *Amitabha Sutra* (or *Shorter Amitabha Sutra*, or *Smaller Sukhavati-Vyuha*, or the *Sutra of Amida*);

b) *Longer Amitabha Sutra* (or *Larger Sukhavati-Vyuha*, or the *Teaching of Infinite Life*);

c) *Meditation Sutra* (or the *Meditation on the Buddha of Infinite Life*, or the *Amitayus Dhyana Sutra*).

Sometimes the last chapter of the *Avatamsaka Sutra* ("The Practices and Vows of the Bodhisattva Samantabhadra") is considered the fourth basic sutra of the Pure Land tradition. Note: in Pure Land, the *Longer Amitabha Sutra* is considered a shorter form of the *Lotus Sutra*.

**Three Treasures (Triple Jewel)** The Buddha, the Dharma and the Sangha (community of monks).

**T'ien T'ai (Tendai) School.** A major school that takes the *Lotus Sutra* as its principal text. Historically, it has had a close relationship with Pure Land. See also "Lotus Sutra."

**Tolerance of Non-Birth.** "Tolerance" (insight) that comes from the knowledge that all phenomena are unborn. Sometimes translated as "insight into the non-origination of all existence/non-origination of the dharmas."

> A Mahayana Buddhist term for the insight into emptiness, the non-origination or birthlessness of things or beings realized by Bodhisattvas who have attained the eighth Stage [Ground] of the path to Buddhahood. When a Bodhisattva realizes this insight he has attained the stage ofnon-retrogression. (Ryukoku University.)

The Pure Land School teaches that anyone reborn in the Pure Land attains the Tolerance of Non-Birth and reaches the stage of non-retrogression, never to fall back into samsara. See also "Non-Birth."

**Transference of Merit.** The concept of merit transference, or sharing one's own merits and virtues with others, is reflected in the following passage:

> Some of us may ask whether the effect of [evil] karma can be ... [changed] by repeating the name of Kuan-Yin. This question is tied up with that of rebirth in Sukhavati [the Pure Land] and it may be answered by saying that invocation of Kuan-Yin's name forms another cause which will right away offset the previous karma. We know, for example, that if there is a dark, heavy cloud above, the chances are that it will rain. But we also know that if a strong wind should blow,

the cloud will be carried away somewhere else and we will not feel the rain. Similarly, the addition of one big factor can alter the whole course of karma ...

It is only by accepting the idea of life as one whole that both Theravadins and Mahayanists can advocate the practice of transference of merit to others. With the case of Kuan-Yin then, by calling on Her name we identify ourselves with Her and as a result of this identification Her merits flow over to us. These merits which are now ours then counterbalance our bad karma and save us from calamity. The law of cause and effect still stands good. All that has happened is that a powerful and immensely good karma has overshadowed the weaker one. (Lecture on Kuan-Yin by Tech Eng Soon - Penang Buddhist Association, c. 1960. Pamphlet.)

**Triple Jewel.** See "Three Treasures."

**Triple Realm (Three Realms, Three Worlds).** The realms of *desire* (our world), *form* (realms of the lesser deities) and *formlessness* (realms of the higher deities). The Western Pure Land is outside the Triple Realm, beyond samsara and retrogression. See also "Pure Land."

**Vaidehi.** The Queen of King Bimbisara of Magadha, India. It was in response to her entreaties that Buddha Shakyamuni preached the *Meditation Sutra*, which teaches a series of sixteen visualizations (of Amitabha Buddha, the Pure Land ...) leading to rebirth in the Land of Ultimate Bliss.

**Vairocana.** The main Buddha in the *Avatamsaka Sutra*. Represents the Dharma Body of Buddha Shakyamuni and all

Buddhas. His Pure Land is the Flower Store World, i.e., the entire cosmos.

**Vimalakirti Sutra.** Also called *Vimalakirti Nirdesa Sutra*. A key Mahayana sutra particularly popular with Zen and to a lesser extent Pure Land followers. The main protagonist is a layman named Vimalakirti who is the equal of many Bodhisattvas in wisdom, eloquence, etc. He explained the teaching of Emptiness in terms of non-duality ... "The true nature of things is beyond the limiting concepts imposed by words." Thus, when asked by Manjusri to define the non-dual Truth, Vimalakirti simply remained silent.

**Virtue.** See "Merit and Virtue."

**Visualization.** See *Meditation Sutra* for explanation.

> The visualizations [in the *Meditation Sutra*] are distinguished into sixteen kinds [shifting from earthly scenes to Pure Land scenes at Visualization 3]: (1) visualization of the sun, (2) visualization of water, (3) visualization of the ground [in the Pure Land], (4) visualization of the trees, (5) visualization of the lake[s], (6) unified visualization of the [50 billion] storied-pavilions, trees, lakes, and so forth, (7) visualization of the [lotus throne of Amitabha Buddha], (8) visualization of the images of the Buddha [Amitabha] and Bodhisattvas [Avalokitesvara and Mahasthamaprapta], (9) visualization of the [Reward body of Amitabha Buddha, i.e., the form in which He appears in the Pure Land], (10) visualization of Avalokitesvara, (11) visualization of Mahasthamaprapta, (12) visualization of one's own rebirth, (13) [see below], (14) visualization of the rebirth of the highest grades,

(15) visualization of the rebirth of the middle grades and (16) visualization of the rebirth of the lowest grades. (K.K. Tanaka, *The Dawn of Chinese Pure Land Doctrine.*)

The 13th Visualization has been summarized as follows:

If one cannot visualize the [Reward body of Amitabha Buddha], focus on the small body, which is sixteen cubits high (the traditional height of Shakyamuni while he dwelt on earth); contemplate an intermingling of the [Reward] and small bodies. (Joji Okazaki, p. 52.)

Visualizations 14-16 refer to the nine lotus grades (of rebirth), divided into three sets of three grades each.

**Way (Path).** The path leading to Supreme Enlightenment, to Buddhahood.

**Wisdom-life.** The life of a Buddha or Bodhisattva, which is sustained by wisdom, just as the life of an ordinary being is sustained by food.

**Yogacara School.** Another name for the Mind-Only school, founded in the fourth century by the brothers Asanga and Vasubandhu.

**Zen.** A major school of Mahayana Buddhism, with several branches. One of its most popular techniques is meditation on koans, which leads to the generation of the Great Doubt. According to this method:

The master gives the student a koan to think about, resolve, and then report back on to the master.

Concentration intensifies as the student first tries to solve the koan intellectually. This initial effort proves impossible, however, for a koan cannot be solved rationally. Indeed, it is a kind of spoof on the human intellect. Concentration and irrationality -- these two elements constitute the characteristic psychic situation that engulfs the student wrestling with a koan. As this persistent effort to concentrate intellectually becomes unbearable, anxiety sets in. The entirety of one's consciousness and psychic life is now filled with one thought. The exertion of the search is like wrestling with a deadly enemy or trying to make one's way through a ring of flames. Such assaults on the fortress of human reason inevitably give rise to a distrust of all rational perception. This gnawing doubt [Great Doubt], combined with a futile search for a way out, creates a state of extreme and intense yearning for deliverance. The state may persist for days, weeks or even years; eventually the tension has to break. (Dumoulin, *Zen Buddhism*, Vol. I, p. 253.)

An interesting koan is the koan of Buddha Recitation. Unlike other koans, it works in two ways. First of all, if a cultivator succeeds in his meditation through this koan, he can achieve awakening as with other koans. However, if he does not succeed, and experience shows that many cultivators do not, then the meditation on the Buddha's name helps him to achieve rebirth in the Pure Land. This is so provided he believes (as most practitioners in Asia do) in Amitabha and the expedient Pure Land. Thus, the Buddha Recitation koan provides a safety net, strengthening the link between Zen and Pure Land.

# Bibliography

Andrews, Allen A., "Nembutsu in Chinese Pure Land Tradition." In *The Eastern Buddhist*, Vol. 3, No. 2, October 1970, p. 20ff.

Asvaghosha, *The Awakening of the Faith*. S. Yoshito Hakeda, tr. New York: Columbia University Press, 1967.

Birnbaum, Raoul, *The Healing Buddha*. Boston, Ma: Shambhala, 1989.

Buzo, Adrian and Tony Prince, tr., *Kyunyo-jon: The Life, Times and Songs of a Tenth Century Korean Monk*. Sydney, Australia: Wild Peony, 1993.

Ch'en, Kenneth K.S., *Buddhism in China: A Historical Survey*. Princeton, NJ: Princeton University Press, 1964.

Chih I (Patriarch), "Ten Doubts about Pure Land." In *Pure Land Buddhism: Dialogues with Ancient Masters*. Master Thích Thiên Tâm, tr. New York: Sutra Translation Committee of the United States and Canada, 1992.

Chihmann (P.C. Lee), tr., *The Two Buddhist Books in Mahayana*. Taipei: Corporate Body of the Buddha Educational Foundation [no date]. Originally published in early 1930's.

Cleary, Thomas, tr., *The Flower Ornament Scripture: A Translation of the Avatamsaka Sutra*. (Three vols.)    Boston, Ma and London: Shambhala,1984-1987.

—— *No Barrier [Wu-men kuan]: Unlocking the Zen Koan*. New York: Bantam, 1993.

Cook, Francis, *Hua-Yen Buddhism: The Jewel Net of Indra*. University Park, Pa and London: Pennsylvania State University Press, 1977.

Crim, Keith, et al., ed., *The Perennial Dictionary of World Religions*. San Francisco, Ca.: Harper & Row, 1989.

*A Dictionary of Buddhism: Chinese-Sanskrit-English-Thai*. Bangkok: The Chinese Budddhist Order of Sangha in Thailand, 1976.

*A Dictionary of Buddhist Terms and Concepts*. Tokyo: Nichiren Shoshu International Center, 1983.

Dumoulin, Heinrich, *Zen Buddhism: A History*. James W. Heisig and Paul Knitter, tr. New York and London: Macmillan, 1988.

Eliade, Mircea, ed., *The Encyclopedia of Religion*. New York: Macmillan.

Fung Yu-Lan, *A History of Chinese Philosophy*. Derk Bodde, tr. Princeton, NJ: Princeton University Press.

Goddard, D., ed., *A Buddhist Bible*. Boston, Ma: Beacon Press, 1970.

Han-Shan Te-Ch'ing, *Pure Land of the Patriarchs: Zen Master Han-Shan on Pure Land Buddhism*. Master Lok To, tr. New York: Sutra Translation Committee of the United States and Canada, 1993.

Hsu, Heng Chi, *What's Buddhism? Theory and Practice*. P.H. Wei, tr. Hong Kong: Hong Kong Buddhist Books Distributor, 1989.

Hsu, Sung-peng, *A Buddhist Leader in Ming China*. University Park, Pa and London: State University of Pennsylvania Press, 1979.

Hsuan Hua (Master), *A General Explanation of the Buddha Speaks of Amitabha Sutra*. San Francisco: Buddhist Text Translation Society, 1974.

Hui Seng, *The Buddha Speaks the Brahma Net Sutra*. Talmadge, Ca: Buddhist Text Translation Society, 1982.

Humphreys, Christmas, *The Buddhist Way of Life*. London: Unwin Paperbacks, 1980. (Originally pub. 1969.)

Hurvitz, Leon, tr., *Scripture of the Lotus Blossom of the Fine Dharma (The Lotus Sutra)*. New York: Columbia University Press, 1976.

Inagaki, Hisao, *A Dictionary of Japanese Buddhist Terms*. Union City, Ca: Heian, 1988.

Kraft, Kenneth, *Zen: Tradition and Transition*. New York: Grove Press, 1988.

Luk, Charles, tr., *The Vimalakirti Nirdesa Sutra*. Boston, Ma: Shambhala, 1972.

Murcott, Susan, *The First Buddhist Women: Translations and Commentary on the Therigatha*. Berkeley, Ca: Parallax Press, 1991.

Narada Maha Thera, *The Buddha and His Teachings*. Singapore: Singapore Buddhist Meditation Centre. (Originally pub. c. 1973.)

Okazaki, Joji, *Pure Land Buddhist Painting*. Elizabeth ten Grotenhuis, tr. Tokyo: Kodansha, 1977.

Price, A.F. and Wong Mou-Lam, tr., *The Diamond Sutra & The Sutra of Hui Neng*. Boston, Ma: Shambhala, 1969.

Prince, A.J. (Tony), "The World of Hua Yen Buddhism." Reprinted in Phât Học (Sepulveda, Ca), No. 6, 1986, p. 135-136.

Red Pine, tr., *The Zen Teaching of Bodhidharma*. Berkeley Ca: North Point Press, 1989.

Sangharakshita, *The Eternal Legacy: An Introduction to the Canonical Literature of Buddhism.* London: Tharpa Publications, 1985.

—— *A Survey of Buddhism: Its Doctrines and methods through the Ages,* 6th printing. London: Tharpa, 1987.

Saso, Michael and David W. Chappell, ed., *Buddhist and Taoist Studies I.* Honolulu: University of Hawaii Press, 1987.

Seki, Hozen, *Buddha Tells of the Infinite: the "Amida Kyo" [Shorter Amitabha Sutra].* New York: American Buddhist Academy, 1973.

*The Shambhala Dictionary of Buddhism and Zen.* Boston, Ma: 1991.

Shih Shing-yun (Master), ed., *Bilingual Buddhist Series.* Taipei: Buddhist Cultural Service, 1962.

Snelling, John, *The Buddhist Handbook: A Complete Guide to Buddhist Schools, Teaching, Practice and History.* Rochester, Vt: Inner Traditions, 1991.

—— *The Elements of Buddhism.* Longmead, England: Element Books, 1990.

Sutra Translation Committee of the United States and Canada, tr., *The Buddhist Liturgy.* 2nd ed. New York, San Francisco, Toronto: 1993.

Suzuki, D. T., "The Development of the Pure Land Doctrine in Buddhism." In *The Eastern Buddhist*, Vol. III, No. 5, Jan.-Mar. 1925.

—— *An Introduction to Zen Buddhism.* New York: Grove Weidenfeld, 1964.

—— "Zen and Jodo, Two Types of Buddhist Experience." In *The Eastern Buddhist*, Vol. IV, No. 2, Jul.-Sept. 1927, p. 89-121.

—— tr., *The Lankavatara Sutra: A Mahayana Text.* Boulder Co: Prajna Press, 1978.

Tay, C.N., "Kuan-Yin: The Cult of Half Asia." In *History of Religions*, Vol. 16, No. 2, Nov. 1975, p. 147-175.

Thích Thiên Tâm (Master), *Buddhism of Wisdom and Faith*, 5th edition. Sutra Translation Committee of the United States and Canada, 1994. (Reprinted by The Corporate Body of the Buddha Educational Foundation, Taipei.)

------, tr., *Pure Land Buddhism: Dialogues with Ancient Masters*. New York: Sutra Translation Committee of the United States and Canada, 1992. (Reprinted by The Corporate Body of the Buddha Educational Foundation, Taipei.)

------ tr., *Pure-Land Zen, Zen Pure-Land: Letters from Patriarch Yin Kuang*. New York: Sutra Translation Committee of the United States and Canada, 1993. (Reprinted by The Corporate Body of the Buddha Educational Foundation, Taipei.)

Thurman, Robert, tr., *The Holy Teaching of Vimalakirti: A Mahayana Scripture*. University Park, Pa and London: Pennsylvania State University Press, 1981.

Watson, Burton, tr., *The Lotus Sutra*. New York: Columbia University Press, 1993.

------, tr., *The Zen Teachings of Master Lin-chi: A Translation of the Lin-chi Lu*. Boston, Ma and London: Shambhala, 1993.

Yü, Chün-fang, *The Renewal of Buddhism in China: Chu-hung and the Late Ming Synthesis*. New York: Columbia University Press, 1981.

# Index

*(Entries in boldface refer to Glossary)*

# A PATH TO TRUE HAPPINESS

**True Sincerity**
*towards others*
**Purity Of Mind**
*within*
**Equality**
*in everything we see*
**Proper Understanding**
*of ourselves and our environment*
**Compassion**
*helping others in a wise and unconditional way*

**See Through**
*to the truth of impermanence*
**Let Go**
*of all wandering thoughts and attachments*
**Freedom**
*of mind and spirit*
**Accord With Conditions**
*go along with the environment*
**Be Mindful Of Amitabha Buddha**
*wishing to reach the Pure Land and follow in*
*His Teachings*

"Wherever the Buddha's teachings have been received, either in cities or countrysides, people would gain inconceivable benefits. The land and people would be enveloped in peace. The sun and moon will shine clear and bright. Wind and rain would appear accordingly, and there will be no disasters. Nations would be prosperous and there would be no use for soldiers or weapons. People would abide by morality and accord with laws. They would be courteous and humble, and everyone would be content without injustices. There would be no thefts or violence. The strong would not dominate the weak and everyone would be settled at their proper place in society."

✸ *The Sutra of Amitabha's Purity, Equality, and Understanding*

# NAME OF SPONSOR

## 助印功德芳名

## 美國淨宗學會

## AMITABHA BUDDHIST SOCIETY OF USA

650 S. BERNARDO AVE. SUNNYVALE, CA 94087, USA
TEL:408-7363386; FAX:408-7363389
http://www.amtb-usa.org

190,000 N.T. Dollars，恭印一萬冊
1999 April, 10000 Copies

# DEDICATION OF MERIT

May the merit and virtue
accrued from this work
adorn the Buddha's Pure Land,
repay the four great kindnesses above,
and relieve the suffering of
those on the three paths below.

May those who see or hear of these efforts
generate Bodhi-mind,
spend their lives devoted to the Buddha Dharma,
and finally be reborn together in
the Land of Ultimate Bliss.
Homage to Amita Buddha!

## NAMO AMITABHA

Reprinted for free distribution by
**The Corporate Body of the Buddha Educational Foundation**
11F., 55 Hang Chow South Road Sec 1, Taipei, Taiwan, R.O.C.
Tel: 886-2-23951198 , Fax: 886-2-23913415
Email: overseas@budaedu.org.tw
http://www.amtb.org.sg ; http://www.amtb.org.tw ;
http://www.amtb-usa.org.
**This book is for free distribution, not to be sold.**
Printed in Taiwan
1999 April, 10000 copies
EN060-1490